Reflecting on

THE SERENITY PRAYER

PHILIP ST. ROMAIN

Liguori

ONE LIGUORI DRIVE
LIGUORI MO 63057-9999
314.464.2500

The Serenity Prayer

God, grant me the serenity
to accept the things I cannot change,
courage to change the things I can,
and the wisdom to know the difference—
living one day at a time,
enjoying one moment at a time,
accepting hardships as the pathway to peace,
taking, as he did, this sinful world as it is,
not as I would have it,
trusting that he will make all things right
if I surrender to his will—
that I may be reasonably happy in this life
and supremely happy with him forever.

❦

Imprimi Potest:
Richard Thibodeau, C.SS.R.
Provincial, Denver Province
The Redemptorists

Imprimatur:
Reverend Monsignor John R. Gaydos
Vicar General, Archdiocese of St. Louis

ISBN 0-7648-0121-X
Library of Congress Catalog Card Number: 97-71702

Scripture quotations are from the *New Revised Standard
Version of the Bible*, copyright © 1989 by the Division of
Christian Education of the National Council of Churches
of Christ in the USA. Used with permission. All rights
reserved.

Cover design by Myra Roth

CONTENTS

Preface

God grant me the wisdom
to accept the things I cannot change,
courage to change the things I can,
and the wisdom to know the difference.

This short prayer has become one of the most cherished in America, if not the whole world. It can be found in forms as diverse as bookmarks, wall plaques, bumper stickers, and collections of inspirational poetry. Millions pray it each day in Twelve-Step recovery meetings, and millions more use it to help sort through the stressful issues in their lives. It summarizes timeless wisdom in just a few words, thus helping both mind and spirit to move more surely into deeper union with God.

Occasionally, one will find a longer version of the prayer:

Living one day at a time,
enjoying one moment at a time,
accepting hardships as the pathway to peace,
taking, as he did, this sinful world as it is,
  not as I would have it,
trusting that he will make all things right
if I surrender to his will—
that I may be reasonably happy in this life
and supremely happy with him forever.

Because these lines don't fit on a bumper sticker, they are not as well known. They are harder to remember and pray than the shorter version. When I first read the longer version, I was immediately struck by its insightfulness and wisdom, so I committed it to memory.

During the past year, as I have written these short chapters, I have done extensive research in libraries and on the Internet, but have yet to come across the full story of this prayer. It is attributed to Reinhold Niebuhr (1892-1971), a Protestant theologian who taught for years at Union Theological Seminary. The opening lines of the prayer form the basis of a homily he gave in 1934. As far as I know, this is the original version of the prayer:

God, give us grace to accept with serenity
the things that cannot be changed,
courage to change the things which should be changed,
and the wisdom to distinguish the one from the other.

I have not been able to find out how the prayer evolved from this formulation (which I like better than the one more commonly used) to its present, simpler wording. Neither have I learned about the origins of the second part of the prayer, which constitutes the so-called longer version.

Nevertheless, my appreciation for this prayer is enormous. After the Lord's Prayer, it is the one that I rely upon most to guide me on the spiritual journey. For this reason, I am happy to help others encounter the wisdom and riches of the Serenity Prayer. May these meditations and the disciplines they suggest lead you to deeper peace and happiness.

PHILIP ST. ROMAIN
October 16, 1996

"Peace I leave with you;
my peace I give to you."
John 14:27

Chapter One
GOD, GRANT ME THE SERENITY

SERENITY IS SUCH a very nice word! It suggests peace, calm, tranquility, and much more. In the Bible, it is *shalom,* a word that is usually interpreted as *peace* but that also connotes *wholeness,* or *fullness of life.* Everybody wants this, but how do we get it?

As the epigraph from John's Gospel affirms, peace is a gift that Christ promises to his followers. Saint Paul also considers it one of the fruits of the Holy Spirit (see Galatians 5:22). Why, then, do so many people seem to lack peace?

I think it is helpful to note that Jesus makes a distinction between two kinds of peace. There is a peace that the world gives; let's call that worldly peace. Then there is the peace that he gives—spiritual peace. Worldly peace is the uneasy truce with fear struck in our hearts when we finally get enough money or gain the approval and admiration of others. It is largely about having and getting. Since it seems that we can never really have absolute financial or relational security, however, worldly peace is always bracketed with anxiety. Even when we come close to realizing it, our minds are still agitated by the thought that we could lose it somehow. Worldly peace can be taken away, and we know it. That is why Jesus contrasts it with spiritual peace, the peace that the world cannot take away.

ALL IS WELL

What, then, is this spiritual peace, shalom, or serenity?

Put simply, it is a deep, inner sense that all is well. The experience goes beyond our systems of emotional or rational intelligence. Rather it is an intuitive or spiritual knowing that produces in us the inner experience of calmness, clarity, and awareness. In serenity, we can live more fully in the now moment, perceiving in acceptance the reality presenting itself without wanting to control things to gratify our selfish desires. There is no need to have or get anything more than what the moment presents; living in serenity itself is sufficient.

Let us consider briefly the powerful testimony of a man who came to know serenity. His name is Bill W., one of the co-founders of Alcoholics Anonymous. Having tried everything to be cured of his alcoholism, he lay on his hospital bed, hopelessly disillusioned about ever feeling well again. His physician, Dr. William Silkworth, had told him that some people he knew were delivered from this addiction through religious faith, but Bill W. was an agnostic who believed that faith in God was incompatible with reason. Besides, he was a stockbroker, a practical man, who knew for a fact that "God helps those who help themselves." Nevertheless, Bill could do nothing more to help himself.

> My depression deepened unbearably and finally it seemed to me as though I were at the bottom of the pit. I still gagged badly on the notion of a Power greater than myself, but finally, just for the moment, the last vestige of my proud obstinacy was crushed. All at once I found myself crying

out, "If there is a God, let Him show Himself! I am ready to do anything, anything!"

Suddenly the room lit up with a great white light. I was caught up into an ecstasy which there are no words to describe. It seemed to me, in the mind's eye, that I was on a mountain and that a wind not of air but of spirit was blowing. And then it burst upon me that I was a free man. Slowly the ecstasy subsided. I lay on the bed, but now for a time I was in another world, a new world of consciousness. All about me and through me there was a wonderful feeling of Presence, and I thought to myself, "So this is the God of the preachers!" A great peace stole over me and I thought, "No matter how wrong things seem to be, they are all right. Things are all right with God and His world."[1]

The experience of Bill W. reminds me of a central theme in Dame Julian of Norwich's visions (or showings, as she called them): all is well. In one of her visions, which were given to her by God, God speaks to her: "All shall be well, and all shall be well, and all manner of things shall be well."[2] All is well in God's world and always will be.

Of course, we know that there is a level at which all is *not* well. People are starving, gangs terrorize our cities, the nations feud, we become sick with all kinds of diseases, we get old and lose our powers, we die. It would be dishonest to deny these realities, and it would be ridiculous to say that they are wonderful. Strategies to obtain worldly peace focus on overcoming these problems or defending ourselves against them somehow. There is no harm in doing everything we can to promote justice and health, of course, just as long as we know that our efforts toward these ends will not give us the peace we so desire. Anything gained through our efforts can be lost in a moment, and we know it. That's why anxiety is never really overcome using strategies for worldly peace.

A TASTE OF HEAVEN

Spiritual peace, then, is not the absence of problems, for we will always have problems. Neither is it the absence of emotional pain, nor the assurance that our prayers will be answered as we would like. As Bill W. and Julian of Norwich show us, spiritual peace is the experiential realization that, amidst the pain and brokenness of our lives, all is well. Our lives are unfolding as they should if we are seeking to walk in union with God. Spiritual peace is the experience of our connection with God whose reign already exists in heaven, even though it has not yet been fully established on earth. Serenity is a taste of heaven on earth: through it, we experience the Spirit of God dwelling in our hearts, giving us the energy to stand on our own two feet and break free from the need to succeed, to impress, to gain power, or to have security. Such peace is the foundation of true love and joy, enabling us to give of ourselves with no thought other than the joy of seeing another grow.

How do we come to know serenity?

The answer is spelled out clearly in the rest of the Serenity Prayer. Serenity is a gift given to us by God, and so it comes to us through our faith relationship with God. Without faith in God, we cannot open ourselves to receive the gifts of God. Faith is more than belief; it is opening ourselves in trust to the One who has created us. It is doing what Bill W. did, as we set aside our pride and rationalism, inviting God to be God for us.

All is well in God's world. When we realize this through our faith connection with God, we experience serenity. We can lose serenity, however, by neglecting to nurture our faith. During such times, we are thrown back upon our own resources. Anxious preoccupation returns along with the willful desire to manipulate the world and other people to conform to our own deluded model of happiness. We need to see how we do this, and we have to give up on worldly peace. We need only return to God, entrusting our lives to God's care, and peace will return in short order. If we do this daily, serenity will grow.

> Do not worry about anything, but in everything by prayer and supplication with thanksgiving let your requests be made known to God. And the peace of God, which surpasses all understanding, will guard your hearts and your minds in Christ Jesus (Philippians 4:6-7).

∽

Reflection and Practice

∼ Do you experience serenity? If so, what is this like for you? If not, was there ever a time when you did? Try to get in touch with an experience of serenity.

∼ How are you trying to create worldly peace for yourself? What consequences do you pay for this effort at self-sufficiency? How is this an obstacle to serenity?

~ How do you experience the connection between faith and serenity?

~ How do you turn your life over to the care of God?

---

1. *Alcoholics Anonymous Comes of Age,* New York: Alcoholics Anonymous World Services, Inc., 1957, p. 12-13. This material is reprinted with the permission of Alcoholics Anonymous World Services, Inc. Permission to reprint this material does not mean that A.A. has reviewed or approved the contents of this publication, nor that A.A. agrees with the views expressed herein. A.A. is a program of recovery from alcoholism only—use of this material in connection with programs and activities which are patterned after A.A., but which address other problems, or in any other non-A.A. context, does not imply otherwise.

2. *The Revelation of Divine Love in Sixteen Showings Made to Dame Julian of Norwich,* translated by M. L. del Mastro, Liguori, MO: Triumph, 1994, p. 102.

Chapter Two

TO ACCEPT THE THINGS
I CANNOT CHANGE

DURING THE SUMMER of 1985, I made an eight-day directed retreat. One of my primary interests was to discern whether I should remain in a secure, well-paying job that was boring me to tears or strike off on my own as a self-employed writer and retreat director. I listed the pros and cons of both choices, envisioned myself in both careers, prayed about it, talked with my spiritual director about it—all to no avail. It seemed that the Spirit wasn't blessing these efforts, since I experienced no definite leanings one way or another. Instead, the primary issues that emerged during the retreat concerned my need to be in control of everything.

My retreat director gave me an exercise that was most beneficial. He asked me to make a list of all the things that contributed to my happiness, and so I did. I wrote down *wife, children, faith in God, physical health, intelligence, money,* and a few other things. I thought about all this for a day or so, then he asked me to examine how much control I had over these various sources of happiness. This was very deflating, but it thoroughly exposed the fears I was dealing with during that period of my life. The truth was, I had no absolute control over any of the things that I had put on my list. For example, my wife and I loved each other: I knew that. But I had no certainty that it would always be that way; I had no control over her love for me, her health, or her survival.

I also did not control my physical or mental health, both of which are dear to me. Faith is a gift given to me by God, and even though I am sure God will not withdraw the gift, I do not control my faith. Money comes and goes. The entire economy can fail, and I will have no say in the matter.

This reflection on my lack of control over the things that gave me happiness thoroughly exposed my worldly or false self. It also frightened me to no end. I remember waking up one night shaking in my bed, terrified to know that I had so little control over anything. My delusions and defenses had been taken away from me, but what was left seemed so fragile and vulnerable that I wasn't sure it was worth it. Unable to sleep and hoping for some relief from my feelings of terror, I went to the chapel to be with the Eucharistic Christ. Often in the past, I had found peace just being with him when I felt anxious. I did feel better after just sitting in silence for a while, but I still felt very fragile. During that period of vulnerability, however, I came to see more clearly than ever that all the things that contributed to my happiness were gifts, not entitlements. I began to feel grateful for these gifts, even though I had no absolute grasp on them. Gratitude restored my sense of serenity and eventually began to produce joy. I had gone through a conversion experience, dying to an old way of being in life and awakening to something I already knew but had not yet surrendered to very deeply.

HUMAN BROKENNESS

Accepting the limitations of our human condition is not an easy matter. Every one of us has been raised in a world of conditional love. We are taught in many ways that our value as human beings depends on what we can do, what we possess, who we know, or how we look. This developmental milieu leaves our minds constantly on the alert for ways to meet the conditions by which we can obtain love and acceptance. We become committed to creating these conditions for ourselves, even if it means becoming dependent on others to do it for us. All these factors contribute to the selfishness and willfulness in everybody. It is the way we compensate for very deep feelings of fear and shame, which are the emotional consequences of being loved conditionally or of being rejected and abused outright.

Unfortunately, we pass on our disease to others by acting it out in many ways. Believing that we are not lovable or acceptable in and of ourselves, we try to create this for ourselves by changing the outside world. We try to use other people to make us happy, and perhaps this works for a while. When they fail to gratify our desires, we try to make them change by criticizing or flattering them, hoping thereby to motivate them through shame and fear to conform with our own model of reality. In addition, we try to impress people in many different ways to get their approval, and when this works we feel better for a little while. When it fails, however, as it eventually does, we feel more inadequate and worthless. These and many other strategies have us trying to compensate for inner feelings of fear and shame. In time, we also add fixes, or mood-altering experiences, to our efforts. Work, TV, junk food, shopping, gambling, alcohol, drugs, relationships, and sex can all function as fixes when we use them to avoid experiencing negative emotions.

I do not intend this short description of our broken human condition to portray a totally negative picture; I only wish to point out that we all suffer from growing up in a world of conditional love. Compulsivity, self-centeredness, attachments, addictions, fear, shame, resentment, broken relationships—these are the fruits of conditional love, which is the same as sin. We cannot be healed of our disease if we do not first acknowledge its existence. Once we have admitted our brokenness, the next step of acceptance makes more sense.

ACCEPTANCE

Accepting the things we cannot change means first and foremost giving up on the project I call "making myself OK." There is no need to do anything or get anything in order to be happy. All our efforts to attain happiness through achievements, relationships, impressing others, and addictive fixes obtain only short-lived results, at best. The restless heart, the troubled memory, the anxious mind—we should not try to change these realities by getting something else (or getting rid of something, for that matter). The person God is creating each of us to be in this moment is already good and is even already happy, so there is no need to do anything to create happiness. Happiness comes of its own accord when we accept the fact that we are completely loved and cared for by God in every moment. There is nowhere to go and nothing to do to become happy. We need only stop disturbing ourselves and happiness will emerge.

Unconditional self-acceptance of the sort I am referring to requires far more than an intellectual affirmation. We must learn to open ourselves again and again to the unconditional love of God. This calls for growth in faith. This also calls for prayer, where we learn to rest in God, allowing the Spirit of God to work within to heal us. We must also stop judging and criticizing ourselves, for this only adds more disharmony to our systems. Instead, we must learn to be gentle with ourselves and allow ourselves plenty of room to make mistakes. It's not a sin to make a mistake; we learn from mistakes.

Acceptance also requires that we embrace the givens of our lives and try to make the best of them. Perhaps we are ill, unemployed, in a troubled marriage, or depressed. Whatever our problems, we will do well to accept them as part of where we are in our journey of life. If our situations can be changed, well that's fine. We can go ahead and work on them. (More on this in the next chapter.) But we should not postpone happiness until these changes come about. No matter what the problem may be, it is possible for us to realize that in this now moment, all is well in God's world. Those who live in union with God come to know this as the great fact of their lives. Frequently, they have more problems than many other people, but their unconditional acceptance of themselves and the meaning of life enables them to make the best of hardship when others would become critical and bitter.

Of course, the hardest part of acceptance is acknowledging that some of the troubling and unpleasant aspects of our lives probably cannot be changed. Accepting self in the light of God's love is especially difficult when we have little hope of changing the situation that pains us. The alternative to doing so is hopelessness and despair, however, which will only add to the burden. For example, if I have a health problem that is seemingly incurable, that is a real cross to bear! But if, in addition, I am also bitter about this problem and become depressed and hopeless about it, I now have another problem—perhaps worse than the first. A negative, judgmental attitude will probably only aggravate the health problem, increasing the pain and adding more fuel to the fires of resentment. This vicious, downward spiral can be broken only if we accept the reality of life—difficult though this may be—without judging, criticizing, or blaming.

Is it possible to do this—to accept an unpleasant situation that we cannot change? Absolutely yes! Not only have I come to do this in several areas of my own life, but I have also observed many other people learning to make the best of very difficult situations. The ultimate witness to this possibility was Jesus Christ, who chose to love and forgive his tormentors even as he hung on the cross. Anyone who would dismiss his example by calling attention to his Sonship with God should consider the examples cited by Viktor Frankl in his powerful little book, *Man's Search for Meaning.* A survivor of Nazi concentration camps, Frankl details the horrible conditions of camp life. Nevertheless, even in such an environment, some were able to maintain their dignity:

> The experiences of camp life show that man does have a choice of action. There were enough examples, often of a heroic nature, which proved that apathy could be overcome, irritability suppressed. Man can preserve a vestige of spiritual freedom, of independence of mind, even in such terrible conditions of psychic and physical stress.
>
> We who lived in concentration camps can remember the men who walked through the huts comforting others, giving away their last piece of bread. They may have been few in number, but they offer sufficient proof that everything can be taken

from a man but one thing: the last of the human freedoms—to choose one's attitude in any given set of circumstances, to choose one's own way.[1]

It is likely that the reader does not have such a difficult situation as did Jesus Christ or Viktor Frankl. If they were able to accept the givens of their situation and make choices to affirm their dignity and that of others, then so can we. The more we come to rest in the conviction of God's unconditional love for us, the easier this becomes. We do not need very much to be happy if God is our pearl of great price, for God is with us always in love.

~

Reflection and Practice

~ How am I trying to make myself OK? What consequences do I experience because of this preoccupation?

~ Do I judge, criticize, and blame other people and circumstances for my unhappiness? What consequences do I experience from this?

~ What are some of the givens of my life that I cannot change but that I would rather not have? How have I been dealing with these issues?

~ What can I do to accept the unpleasant givens of my life that cannot be changed?

---

1. Viktor E. Frankl, *Man's Search for Meaning: An Introduction to Logotherapy*, New York: Pocket Books, 1959, pp. 103-104.

Chapter Three

COURAGE TO CHANGE
THE THINGS I CAN

"COURAGE IS FEAR that has said its prayers." So reads a plaque one of our daughters gave to my wife several years ago. I like this saying very much, for it seems to capture the essence of what courage is all about.

Fear is the dark poison in the souls of all who have not come into the fullness of union with God. Early in life, we become fearful as a consequence of being loved conditionally. "Perfect love casts out fear," notes 1 John 4:18. When we are loved imperfectly, or conditionally, fear comes into our lives. To compensate for this fear we develop a split self, showing one face to the outside world while experiencing a different reality within. We develop defenses to keep this fear out of awareness, and we begin to pursue worldly peace to gratify our dis-ease. Such pursuits bring only short-term pleasure or relief, however, thus deepening the fear within.

Most people experience fear about many things. Indeed, so accustomed are we to living with fear that we might think this to be the normal state of humanity. After all, it seems that everyone else fears the same things we do.

Well…not quite everyone!

There are people who seem to be generally oblivious to fear. I'm not speaking here of daredevils who put their lives on the line to demonstrate their skill in racing, or balancing on a tightrope, or other risky pursuits. Daredevils have the utmost confidence in their skill, but they are often afraid of failure. Some, too, have lost reverence for their lives, and so their daring is a quasi-suicidal act. The kinds of fearless people I'm talking about are the saints and mystics of the world, who have come to know the perfect Love that casts out all fear. However, their journey to serenity has not been an escape from fear, as is the journey in pursuit of worldly peace. Rather, their journey to serenity is a journey *through* fear.

This point is most important. We do not conquer our fears by avoiding them or distracting ourselves from them. We conquer a fear by facing whatever it is we would like to avoid, by feeling the emotions, and by acting courageously in the face of this fear. By doing this again and again, we eventually overcome our fears. The problem, of course, is that none of us wants to do this work.

FACING YOUR FEARS

What are your fears? Can you name them? The more specific you can be in identifying your fears and anxieties, the better.

Let's look at a list of common fears:

- the disapproval of others
- making mistakes
- failure
- sickness
- loss of a loved one
- economic hardship
- loss of a job
- death

These are the most common fears of the human race. If humanity could be free of these fears, how wonderful it would be! Perhaps you have other fears as well. Go ahead and write them down. Make as complete and honest a list as possible. This is the first step to staring your fears in the face.

The next step is to determine which of your fears has been most prevalent lately. This might not be easy to do, since fear has a way of coming out in many places at once. Pick only one fear, however, and reflect on these questions:

- When do I experience this fear? (Recall specific episodes, and even allow yourself to experience the emotions connected with them.)
- How does this fear limit my experience of life? In other words, how does this fear limit the kinds of choices I make?
- What other consequences do I experience because of this fear?

These three questions enable you to see how fear works in your life. Take each of your fears, and examine them in the light of these questions. This practice alone will bring you relief, for fear cannot grow when the mind becomes more aware.

After you complete the steps recommended above, you will be ready to actually encounter the more fearful aspects of your life. You do not have to go out of your way to do this. Opportunities will arise, and when they come, you will either think and act as you always have before, enabling fear to grow, or you will do something different and creative, diminishing the amount of fear in your life.

Where do we find the courage to encounter the fearful and then act differently?

"Courage is fear that has said its prayers."

This might sound simplistic, but remember that perfect Love alone casts out all fear. And we find such perfect Love only in God. Just as serenity and acceptance have their root and foundation in faith and prayer, so, too, does courage.

ACTING COURAGEOUSLY

Courage has two aspects. One is a passive aspect— a gift of the Holy Spirit. This means that those who grow closer to God, especially through prayer, will find themselves inspired and emboldened at times to act courageously. Thus were the fearful apostles able to stand before throngs on Pentecost Sunday and proclaim the gospel when, a few hours earlier, they were hiding from everyone. The old spiritual manuals spoke of such courage as an infused gift of the Spirit, meaning that it is poured into our hearts by God and is not an achievement on our part. If you need this gift, you can ask God to give it to you.

The other aspect of courage is a virtue. It is an active discipline that you must put into practice. This means that even if you do not feel inspired or emboldened to act in a way different from what fear dictates, you must make the effort to do so anyway. Such acts of courage undertaken through the weeks and months will slowly whittle away your fears. Your courageous acts also make it possible for the infused gift of courage to be given to you more fully.

Courageous acts need not be earthshaking, although even the smallest of such deeds contributes to changing the world. As this part of the Serenity Prayer states, you only need to act to change the things you can. When you examined your fears, you undoubtedly noted many specific examples of things that can be changed. Acting courageously means deliberately choosing to go against your fear by choosing a more rational and creative course of action. Here are a few examples of what I mean:

- taking the first step to reconcile with someone you're not getting along with
- getting up a little earlier to take time for prayer
- confronting someone whose behavior bothers you
- refusing to indulge in gossip
- choosing to get help for an emotional or relational problem

This list could go on, of course, but the point is for you to make your own list. If you're not sure where to start, remember that even though it is not always possible to change the outside world, it is almost always possible to change your attitude in a given situation. This is one of the greatest powers given to human beings—the freedom to choose the way we think about the events and situations of our lives. If you begin to exercise this power more fully, you will experience more energy, joy, and serenity. You will feel less controlled by other people and external circumstances. You will have come to realize that happiness is a state of mind and not a consequence of getting and having the right things or of being in control.

Of course, the greatest obstacles to choosing your attitude are the unconscious habits of thought already operating in your mind. These robotic thought habits have been developed through years of thinking and choosing, and so they are rooted deeply within. It takes courage to examine them, which is why so many people do not even bother. They're afraid of what they'll find if they begin to reflect on their attitudes and motives, and they don't want to lose the precarious sense of self they've developed through the years. However, any self that can be lost through honest reflection is not the true self. It is only a delusional fabrication created by the mind to compensate for fear.

The spiritual life is a struggle to become completely authentic—who you really are—in the light of God's unconditional love for you. This takes courage, but it is well worth the risks.

∾

Reflection and Practice

∼ "Take courage; I have conquered the world," says the Lord (John 16:33). Are you ready to wake up and live? What, if anything, might be holding you back?

∼ Complete the reflection exercises suggested in this chapter to help you name your fears so you can see how they limit your experience of life.

∼ Make a list of ways you can act more courageously. Ask someone you trust to hold you accountable for acting this way.

∼ Pray for the gift of courage, and believe that God has given it to you.

Chapter Four

AND THE WISDOM
TO KNOW THE DIFFERENCE

THIS WISDOM IS the ability to discern which things we cannot change and which things we can. Such wisdom moves us to acceptance of the non-negotiable aspects of life, and it also gives us the courage to act when and as we must. Wisdom of this sort is eminently practical, informing decisions made in everyday life.

How do we get this wisdom?

The first way comes from life experience. Sometimes there is just no knowing what we can change and what we cannot without stepping out into the unknown and doing something. If things work out, fine; if not, we still learn lessons that can inform our next decisions.

For example, I have often struggled with the issue of acceptance versus control in my relationships with others. As a parent, in particular, I feel obligated to try to influence my children in certain ways. I want them to learn to be responsible, so I give them chores to do. It is unacceptable to me if they fail to do them (unless they have a good excuse). What should I do when they don't do their chores? Accept this as something I cannot change and let them off the hook? Or nag them and threaten them until they do their work?

The answer is a little of both: I need to accept the fact that kids will be kids and not make a federal case out of their lapses in responsibility. After all, this is how I behaved when I was younger (and, truth be told, I still act this way at times). But I also need to continue to try to influence them to adopt more disciplined behavior. If I don't do this, and they leave our home without such habits, it will go badly for them as adults. And so I do enforce consequences for work not done, and at times, I even remind them when I really need the chore done on time. Wisdom, in this case, involves both accepting the parts of the situation that I cannot change and continuing to hang in there with the parts that I can. It seems to me that, more often than not, this both/and approach is how things go. Wisdom must take into account the both/and situations of life in addition to the either/or.

WISDOM AND DETACHMENT

Practical wisdom presupposes that we are somewhat detached in our approach to a situation. Detachment is often misunderstood as passivity or indifference, but true detachment means that we must be willing to act if necessary or to draw back if that is better. We must want what is good to come out of a situation and not try to manipulate things to achieve a certain end.

What frustrates our growth in wisdom most is the absence of this detachment. We generally *do* want things to come out a certain way, and we manipulate to realize our desires, for example pleasure, security, power, wealth, approval, and other such worldly values. We might bring an extraordinary amount of intelligence and even cleverness to bear in realizing these desires, but this is not the same thing as wisdom.

For example, there are many people who have learned how to walk along the edges of the law in order to enrich themselves financially. A lawyer I know works with corporations to help them do this (and he himself has made a mint because of his services). The overwhelming concern here is not what is right but what is legally permitted. The motivation driving him and these companies is to make as much money as possible within the limits of the law. This might not seem so bad, but it will never lead to growth in wisdom.

We see detachment at work in the life of Jesus in the Garden of Gethsemane. Realizing that the authorities were plotting against him, he prays: "Father, if you are willing, remove this cup from me; yet, not my will but yours be done" (Luke 22:42). Jesus had a preference that he be spared the cup of torture and death. We can all relate to this. But his desire to do the will of the Father was stronger than his preference. His love of the Father enabled him to truly say, "not my will but yours be done." This is perfect detachment—the willingness to suffer even unto death if that is what love calls for.

We see from this example that there is nothing wrong with having preferences or even praying that they be realized. It is natural to prefer health over sickness, riches over poverty, and so forth. Is our desire to do God's will stronger than any other preference, however? If it is not, then we will be limited in our growth in wisdom (and serenity, love, and joy as well). Only this desire to love God with our whole heart, soul, mind, and strength will enable us to realize the detachment that leads to wisdom. Granted, we will do this imperfectly sometimes; nevertheless, it is progress in this primary intention that is important, not perfection.

SACRED WISDOM

Just as courage can be either an acquired virtue or an infused gift, so, too, is wisdom. The practical wisdom discussed so far is a consequence of our own experiences in detached loving. This is real wisdom that can grow through time and bear wonderful fruit.

There is another kind of wisdom spoken of in Scripture, however, the Wisdom that is the Spirit of God herself. In the Hebrew Scriptures, Wisdom (*Sophia*) is personified in the feminine aspect. Proverbs, Wisdom, and Sirach sing her praises. For example:

> *She is a breath of the power of God,*
> *and a pure emanation of the glory of*
> *   the Almighty;*
> *therefore nothing defiled gains entrance*
> *   into her.*
> *For she is a reflection of eternal light,*
> *a spotless mirror of the working of God,*
> *and an image of his goodness.*
> *Although she is but one, she can do all things,*
> *and while remaining in herself, she renews*
> *   all things.*

Wisdom 7:25-27

Later, the prophet Isaiah will speak of the Spirit of God blessing the followers of the offshoot of Jesse with

> *the spirit of wisdom and understanding,*
> *the spirit of counsel and might,*
> *the spirit of knowledge and the fear of the LORD.*

Isaiah 11:2

Thus does the Spirit of Wisdom of the Hebrew Scriptures become identified with the Holy Spirit poured out on the Church at Pentecost.

Just as we can pray for the gift of courage, we can

pray for the Spirit of Wisdom to be poured out in our hearts. God wants to share this Wisdom with us:

> *To those without sense she says,*
> *"Come, eat of my bread*
> *   and drink of the wine I have mixed.*
> *Lay aside immaturity, and live,*
> *   and walk in the way of insight."*
>
> Proverbs 9:4-6

Then there is the promise of Jesus:

Ask, and it will be given you; search, and you will find; knock, and the door will be opened for you. For everyone who asks receives, and everyone who searches finds, and for everyone who knocks, the door will be opened....If you then, who are evil, know how to give good gifts to your children, how much more will the heavenly Father give the Holy Spirit to those who ask him! (Luke 11:9-13).

We can pray for the Holy Spirit of Wisdom to be given to us. In fact, the closer we draw to God in prayer, the more this sacred Wisdom will rub off on us. Many of the saints and mystics were accomplished theologians even though they never had much academic training. They learned the ways of God from Wisdom herself, who is surely the best of all teachers!

GROWING IN WISDOM

Although practical wisdom is different from the Wisdom that is the Spirit of God, they are related.

Supernatural Wisdom cannot be grasped with the human intellect and will, but those who grow in practical wisdom are disposed to receiving supernatural Wisdom from God. We human beings are created in God's image and likeness. To the extent that we use our human powers to image the divine reality, we are capable of receiving the graces that transform us into a likeness of God. If we love human beings, we open ourselves to receiving divine Love and, in turn, loving with this divine Energy as well. Likewise, if we practice loving detachment in our discernments and deliberations, we dispose ourselves to receiving the Wisdom from on high. This Wisdom becomes increasingly available to guide us in the everyday affairs of life, providing we continue to live in loving detachment. This is how we bring the goodness and love of God into our world today.

Reflection and Practice

~ What kinds of motives generally guide your decision-making? How detached are you from having things come out your way?

~ How strong is your intention to do God's will in all things? What consequences do you experience when this is your primary intention? What happens when other intentions and motives predominate?

~ When you have a difficult decision to make, become as detached from a particular course of action as possible, then pray that God will illuminate your conscience with the gift of Wisdom. After doing so, trust that the leanings of your heart manifest the guidance of Wisdom, and act accordingly. It works!

Chapter Five
LIVING ONE DAY AT A TIME

"ONE DAY AT a time" is a favorite slogan of people in recovery from addiction. During the years when I worked as a substance abuse counselor, I came to see the wisdom of this saying. Many times, the person in recovery is worried about staying sober for the rest of his or her life. The motivation to do so is there, but the future seems to be overwhelmingly large and doubtful; staying sober forever seems an impossible resolution to fulfill. The wise counsel of Alcoholics Anonymous is to recognize that although no one can guarantee anything forever, life is much more manageable if lived one day at a time. The challenge for today is to stay sober and live the day as fully as possible. This advice is usually accepted in gratitude! Anyone who manages to stay sober each day will also fulfill the goal of perpetual sobriety—one day at a time.

This is not simply a clinical strategy relevant only for people in recovery from an addiction. In the Gospel of Matthew (6:34), we hear Jesus saying, "So do not worry about tomorrow, for tomorrow will bring worries of its own. Today's trouble is enough for today." Jesus is not encouraging us to avoid setting goals and making plans, nor is he advocating that we live only for today. Planning for the future is a good and healthy discipline. Notice that what he is discouraging is worry about the future. This was the problem with the people in recovery with whom I worked, and it is an affliction that burdens most of us from time to time.

DAILY RHYTHM

There is no doubt in my mind that most of us have lost touch with our daily rhythms. We have produced a technological culture that is synchronized to "clock time" and have committed ourselves to caring for this technology according to its own temporal rhythms. We work eight-hour days governed by the clock, we eat by the clock, and we take breaks by the clock. Indeed, one of the great stressors of our day is time stress. More heart attacks happen on Monday mornings than at any other time. The reason for this is obvious.

The notion of absolute mental control—mind over matter—is a delusion. We believe we ought to be able to discipline ourselves into doing the kinds of jobs we do at the times we do them without negative consequences to our bodies. Mind over matter is a reality, but for us human beings, there is no mind without matter. Our natural biological rhythms are violated daily by the demands we place on ourselves. For example, research has shown that most people don't sleep enough and that they sleep poorly. This alone is enough to damage a person's health. In addition, it seems natural for humans to have a nap in the afternoon. Many cultures provide for this. Not so in America where machine time reigns.

Each person has a unique daily rhythm of sleeping, waking, eating, working, and so forth. Some do well with breakfast right away; others must wait awhile before eating. Living by the clock makes it impossible for us to honor these rhythms. The rhythms of nature are also built into our systems. We need fresh air, sunshine, and contact with nature to be fully human. Instead, most of us today breathe in pollution and spend more time in front of the television than outside.

Recovering the fullness of our humanity requires that we do as much as possible to honor our daily rhythms. Getting enough sleep and eating properly help to provide a sound biological foundation for spiritual growth. Contact with nature and attention to the needs of the body are essential. Being in touch with daily rhythms is a prerequisite for recovering inner wisdom. We are not minds without matter. As one friend of mine put it, "matter matters." Mind affects the matter of the body in ways we are just beginning to understand.

SCATTERED LIVING

As human beings with a spiritual consciousness, it is possible for us to be aware of the past and the future. This is not the case with other animals, whose consciousness is primarily sensory and instinctual. A cat will become alert and anxious when a dog walks by, but several minutes later, when the dog is gone, the cat will be sleeping soundly. Out of sight, out of mind: that's how it goes for animals. Not so for human beings, however. If we are insulted by another, we may find ourselves mulling over this hours and even days after the incident happens. We think of what we could have said as a comeback, thus living in the past; we fantasize what we will say and do when we meet this person again, projecting our consciousness into the future. In either case, the emotional consequences of the unhappy encounter drive our consciousness, contaminating our experience of the present moment with distorting thoughts and fantasies. We project out of our emotion, and we do it every day. This is what the mystics mean when they say that most people live in a state of delusion.

The first way to get out of this is to acknowledge

what is going on. We have already emphasized this in earlier chapters, but the point needs to be constantly underscored. "What am I doing?" is one of the best questions we can ask ourselves all throughout the day. "I'm thinking about what to say to Joe when I see him again; I'll really let him have it!" Easy enough so far. What we must now recognize is that whatever we give attention to, we energize. If I give attention to getting revenge against Joe, I increase my anger toward him and accelerate the flow of troubling thoughts in my mind. The problem is that once we have given lots of attention and energy to a particular concern, it takes on a life of its own. It continues working within us even after we decide we don't want it to be that way. Thoughts and the emotional energies they carry cannot be stopped by a simple act of will power, just as we cannot make a car going sixty miles per hour stop on a dime. Thoughts and emotions have a momentum that keeps them going for a while, the duration of which depends on how much energy and attention we have invested in them through the days. This is what the Hindus mean by *karma*.

Whenever we come into silence, we experience the momentum of our fragmented thoughts. This is unpleasant, and it is one reason why many people avoid silence—especially prayer. Rather than face themselves in the silence, many create a noisy environment outside of themselves to match their inner fragmentation. For example, I know people who turn on the television or radio as soon as they wake up. They drive to work with the radio on, and they keep their minds busy with the affairs of everyday life all through the day. Meanwhile, below the surface currents of mental activity, deep currents of thought and emotion continue to work— sometimes to destruction.

Inevitably, every thought and emotion affects the body. During the past few years, scientists have identified a class of biochemicals called peptides. These are the chemical equivalent of thoughts. Every cell in our body has thousands of receptor sites for these peptides. When the mind is thinking, "I just don't know if I can get through this day, I feel so down," this stimulates the production of peptides that communicate a chemical equivalent of this message to every cell in our bodies. Imagine, now, your liver or your immune system "thinking" this same message. The discovery of peptides has helped us to understand why mental and physical health go hand in hand.

Just as thoughts and emotions eventually have a momentum that is difficult to reverse, so, too, does the health of the body. When the organ systems of the body have been conditioned in negative, depressing energies, they begin to function that way habitually. This is why it is so hard for people to diet or sustain a program of exercise. It's like trying to stop that speeding car on a dime. Eventually, the momentum of unhealthy living makes a greater claim on our will than do our good resolutions, and we are back to eating junk food and lounging around. This should not surprise us, nor should it discourage us when it happens. Reversing this situation will call forth the acceptance, courage, and wisdom discussed in earlier chapters, as well as the discipline of daily living that is our concern here.

DAILY RESOLUTIONS

We can't stay sober forever, or diet forever, or do anything forever—not even stay married to the same person. *But we can do what we can do today.* Furthermore, we can do what must be done today as best we can without having to do it perfectly. What is important is progress, not perfection. If we can slow the momentum of unhealthy living from sixty miles per hour to fifty-nine miles per hour, that's progress! If we do this every day, then sooner or later we will be living a much healthier life.

So what, practically, can you do today?

This is where the keep-it-simple slogans of recovery groups are helpful. You've already gotten in touch with some of the things about your life that you can change, so begin to put them into practice. This means doing less of what hurts you and more of what you know can help you.

For example, do you smoke cigarettes? Smoke less today. Eat junk food? Eat less today. If you can avoid both completely for today, that is better, but less is progress, too.

How about healthy practices? Do you exercise? If not, give it at least five minutes. Take time for prayer? Start with five minutes. Is your marriage hurting? Argue less today, and do something kind for your spouse. Start putting something into your system to begin building a momentum of healthy energies. That's all you have to do every day. The hardest part is starting because the momentum of negative energies can be so strong.

A few healthy practices each day can contribute enormously to your sense of health and well-being. Health is normal; sickness is not. Every level of our being was created to know and experience the happiness that God has for us. Healthy peptides have great power in rejuvenating our cells, and organ systems invested with a momentum of "I can do this" hardly ever get sick. Good is stronger than evil. We can actually experience this good news in our bodies.

TIME MANAGEMENT

Several years ago, when I became self-employed, I fell into the trap of "time is money." Faced with financial pressures and a family to raise, I tried to do as much in my business as I could each day. Like almost everyone else, I was raised with the slogan, "Never put off until tomorrow what you can do today." The problem with this is that self-employed people are never finished with their work, and the more they do today, the more money they make. This went well for a while, but then I began to feel distant from my wife and children. I also began to sleep poorly, so preoccupied had I become about finances and work. Eventually, my enthusiasm for almost everything was diminishing; I was burning out.

At about that time, and seemingly out of the blue, a friend said something to me that was surely inspired by God. As I related to him how much I had going on, he listened sympathetically, then told me that I needed to be careful about doing too much. I knew this, of course; in fact, I taught this in some of my stress management classes. What was significant was that I *heard* him, and I knew it was true for me.

As a result of this encounter, I changed my approach. I went home, got a sheet of paper, and made the following columns:

<u>Things to do</u>   <u>Date to be completed</u>   <u>Hours needed</u>

I filled out the list as completely as I could for every task I had to do. This got everything out of my head, so I didn't have to keep thinking about it.

Next, I looked at this list and was able to identify

what needed to be done the next day. I set for myself an eight-hour workday, and each day I accomplished the tasks for that day. If there was time left over, and I felt inclined to do more during my eight hours, I did so. Eventually, in my stress management workshops, I began to teach a new slogan: *"Never do today what can be put off until tomorrow—unless it will be fun to do it."* This is not a recipe for laziness and procrastination. We do today what must be done, just as the Lord encourages: "Today's trouble is enough for today" (Matthew 6:34). And today's work is enough for today.

Of course, there are some people whose problem is the opposite of my own. There really are procrastinators and couch potatoes among us. Such people can also benefit from the exercise I am recommending. Make your list and see what must be done, then do it. Do no more unless you really want to, but at least do what you must. To do otherwise is to sink into the momentum of sluggishness and negativity.

Reflection and Practice

~ Are you a person who generally tries to do too much during a day or too little? Try working the time management suggestion described in this chapter.

~ What is one unhealthy thing you can do less of today? What is one healthy practice you can do more of?

~ How does your daily schedule effect your experience of daily rhythms?

~ What can you do to become more in touch with your natural daily rhythms?

Chapter Six

ENJOYING ONE MOMENT
AT A TIME

WE CAN EXPERIENCE our spiritual nature in one important way through our experience of time. As we discussed in the last chapter, animals live completely in
the present moment. They don't worry about the future
or harbor grudges. As they go about responding to the
circumstances of the moment, they develop a set of conditioned responses that they bring into the next moment,
and the next, and so on. We, too, bring our conditioning into each moment, but we also possess the ability
to consciously recall a past incident and to dream of
future possibilities. Although we live in space and time,
there is a dimension of our awareness capable of stand-
ing outside of space and time, from which vantage point
we can regard past and future as though they were taking place in this moment.

This spiritual dimension of awareness is a great gift
to us. Because we can reflect on the past and actually
relive many experiences, we are able to learn from the
past and, like our Lady, treasure its memories in our
hearts (see Luke 2:51). We can also envision ourselves
moving into a future. Those who work to stimulate personal growth appreciate this power more and more. If
we cannot see ourselves doing something, there is little
chance that we will ever be able to do it. The discipline
of creative visualization is one way to reverse this ten-
dency; by envisioning positive outcomes, we actually

move our energies in the direction of fulfilling what we have seen. So it is perfectly natural for us to remember the past and to envision the future; the spiritual nature of human consciousness makes this possible for us, and there is nothing wrong with doing so.

THREE EXPERIENCES OF TIME

Time is an interesting phenomenon—something that physicists have puzzled over for decades. What concerns us here is not a scientific understanding of time but our experience of it. There are three possibilities.

The first and most common experience people have is of time as *linear*. This is sometimes called horizontal or chronological time and refers to our experience of time as a movement from past to future. Our recognition that things have a beginning and an end is an example of this. Knowing this, we experience our lives to be unfolding from our conception toward our death, and this gives us a sense of being on a time line. Time seems to have a quantitative dimension. If we are young, we believe we have plenty of time left to live, and we don't think much about death. If we are old, we might feel that we are running out of time, and depending on how we have lived our lives, we feel happy or sad about time. Then there are all the other time lines that stress or excite us. We might look forward to a celebration, but we might also dread Monday morning and going back to work; we might eagerly anticipate a visit with a friend, but we might also dread a scheduled confrontation.

Our capacity to experience time as linear is a great gift that enables us to remember where we have come from and to plan where we would like to go. The downside is that linear time also contributes to time stress. Because linear time is measurable, we can feel as though we are up against time or running out of time. How many people today complain about not having enough time to do what they want to do? The rat race in which so many are caught is thoroughly suffused with time stress. People feel their lives moving from the past into a future that doesn't seem to have enough time. You can see it in their eyes and their nonverbal expressions. They are distracted and preoccupied; they are here but not present, on the go but not really living. If the days could be lengthened to thirty-six hours, their suffering would not be alleviated, for they would simply fill it up with more things to do. They are "human-doings," not human beings, and they never have enough time to do all they think they need to do to be happy.

Our second experience of time can also be positive or negative. *Chairotic* (ky rot' ik) *time* refers to our experience of *seasons of time*. For example, we experience childhood, adolescence, young adulthood, and so on. We experience spring, summer, fall, and winter. These seasons of time are comprised of many moments of linear time, but each season has a feeling about it that we hold in memory in a special way. Furthermore, we each have our unique seasons. People who move from one place to the next will experience these as distinct periods in their lives; others may remember changing jobs, divorce, or a prolonged illness as a special season of life.

In many ways, chairotic time is a higher spiritual experience than linear time, for it enables us to stand outside of time (time-transcendence) to understand our lives. We can even reenter an earlier season for a brief period and thus experientially contrast where we were then with our present situation. This has happened to me many times as I have listened to music. A particular song will trigger a memory, and for a brief period I will feel myself as I was when I listened to the same song years ago. A flood of memories and feelings from that time in life will come, and if I consent to them, I can reexperience the person I was then. Generally, I am grateful for these chairotic memories and sometimes even nostalgic for the good old days. They always bring the gift of enabling me to see how my life has changed.

Chairotic experiences might not always be pleasant, however. Sometimes a season has much pain and suffering, so much so that we would just as soon forget that it ever happened. We might avoid anyone or anything that could remind us of that time, or we might develop inner defenses to wall off those memories. This is sometimes necessary, but in the long run, it is unhealthy. Remembering unhealthy seasons in our lives can be a great learning experience if we are prepared to do so or if we have the support of a counselor. How did this time affect us? What lessons—healthy and unhealthy—did we learn? How has this period affected the way we open ourselves to emotional experience now? Eventually, we need to re-claim the seasons of our lives, whether they were pleasant or not. Chairotic time gives us a sense of the story of our lives. What good is a story if we leave out important chapters?

The third kind of time is *eternal life.* Many people read about eternal life in Scripture and interpret it as unending existence. And so it is. In terms of time, however, the experience is not one of having an ulimited quantity of time, extending linear time into infinity. Rather, it is entering into *God's own experience of time,* which theologians call "the ever-present Now." Chairotic time gives us a small taste of how vast periods can be present to us in a given moment, and so we can intuit from this something of what all of time is for God. Being totally spiritual, God's awareness transcends matter and is not in any way determined by space and time. God does not experience linear time, but everything that unfolds in linear time is present to God. So are all the chairotic seasons of our lives and seasons of the universes. Time is real, but for God, time is never before and after, only Now. Some have called this "vertical time," as opposed to the horizontal dimension of linear time. If we were to draw it out, we might do so as follows:

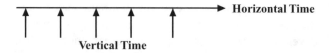

Notice that vertical time intersects every point on the horizontal time line. Each point of intersection is a Now-moment. From the perspective of God, all moments in linear time are always known. Because we live in space and time, however, we experience linear time and the seasons of our lives as an unfolding process. With proper attentiveness to the present moment, however, we can also begin to get a glimpse of the experience of eternal life.

ATTENTIVE LIVING

To get an idea of what the experience of eternal life is like, consider a time recently when you really enjoyed yourself. Maybe it was a movie or a visit with a friend. During such a period, did it not seem as though time did not exist? "Time flies when you're having fun" goes the old saying. Of course, there was linear time plodding away, and eventually you had to leave the experience and go on to something else. If that something else was an unpleasant task, you probably became very conscious of time and began to look at your watch frequently.

What does all this tell us about time and attention? The most obvious conclusion is that time seems to go slowly when we're unhappy with what we're doing and seems to disappear when we're thoroughly enjoying ourselves. The difference between these two experiences has nothing to do with time itself, but it has everything to do with how we are *in* time. When we enjoy ourselves, we are un–self-conscious: we aren't thinking much about ourselves because we're too busy experiencing the life that is happening. The self is there, of course, but we are not reflecting on it. When the experience is over and we reflect on it, we note how we were feeling and thinking and thus relive something of the experience (chairotic time). While it is happening, however, it seems as though there is no-self and no-time.

These common experiences of enjoyment give us a taste of what eternal life is like. We note two essential characteristics of the experience. One, as we have already mentioned, is that the self is not reflecting on its experiences but is so actively engaged in the moment as to be un–self-conscious. This very well describes God's basic attitude, which theologians tell us is Self-Transcending Love. To experience this, however, we must be completely open to the gift of the moment, and this is the second characteristic. We must be here now, without past or future interfering. Horizontal and vertical time meet in a now moment, and so the eternal dimension of time can only be experienced when we have dropped the past and quit projecting into the future. This is the hard part.

Dropping the past does not mean that we forget it but that we quit acting in compensation for past hurts. Past hurts keep some of our attention in the past and cause us to anxiously project negative possibilities into the future (and thus, perhaps, bring them to pass). We can never fully surrender into the now of life as long as such past hurts weigh us down. We can know occasional moments of freedom from self-concern, and that can spur us onward. Living fully in the present requires complete healing of the past, however.

A simple discipline, then, is to strive to *be here now in love.* Each moment presents a new and unique inter-section between vertical and horizontal time, which the spiritual nature of human consciousness is privileged to experience. The present moment is where life is really happening; if we are not here, then we miss life. We can live in the now-moment only when our attitude is that of being-in-love. Otherwise we approach the moment with defenses and expectations that turn our experience of time into a linear or chairotic experience. By *love* I mean that we must be open to receiving what the moment has to offer and willing to give in return what is required of us. It is natural and unavoidable for us to bring to each moment our expectations of what we would like to have happen; but we must hold these expectations lightly and be willing to surrender them if the needs of love so require. Only those who love in this manner can experience eternal life. Is this not the essence of the good news?

Some will object that being here now in love sounds imprudent or irresponsible. After all, should we not plan our lives more carefully and take the time to remember lessons learned? If the present moment calls for planning and remembering, then that is what we must do. There is no conflict between planning or remembering and being here now in love. Even time management does not conflict with living fully in the present moment. The point is to bring our full attention to whatever it is we are doing, rather than being scattered all over the place:

> I say: "What are you doing at this moment, Zorba?" "I'm sleeping." "Well, sleep well...." "What are you doing at this moment, Zorba?" "I'm kissing a woman." "Well, kiss her well, Zorba! And forget all the rest while you're doing it; there's nothing else on earth, only you and her!"[1]

Zorba has the right spirit! Whatever it is you're doing, try to do it as attentively and lovingly as possible. Attention is the spiritual muscle of the soul, and it must grow stronger if the soul is to know eternal life. When attention is scattered, the moment is missed and eternal life is lost.

When the enjoyable experience of time that captivates us is the divine presence, we come to know most purely the meaning of eternal life. Consider, for example, the experience of J. Krishnamurti recounted below:

> There was, as one woke up this morning early, a flash of "seeing," "looking," that seems to be going on and on forever. It started nowhere and went nowhere but in that seeing all sight was included and all things. It was a sight that went beyond the streams, the hills, the mountains, past the earth and the horizon and the people. In this seeing there

was penetrating light and incredible swiftness. The brain could not follow it nor could the mind contain it. It was pure light and a swiftness that knew no resistance.[2]

This seeing and looking Krishnamurti describes comprise the consciousness of eternal life. It transcends our ordinary psychological experience of time; it is our destiny to know this reality always.

~

Reflection and Practice

~ Draw a time line representing the years from your birth to the present, marking off what you would consider the major periods or seasons of your life. Give a title to each season and a few characteristics of each.

~ What kind of a feel for time do you generally have?

~ On what occasions in your life have you experienced time flying? What was it about those experiences that helped you break free from time stress?

~ How do you generally deal with time stress?

~ Make a commitment to be here now in love. Notice whenever your attention strays from this attitude, and call it back. Let this be the primary focus of your time in prayer and meditation.

---

1. Nikos Kazantzakis, *Zorba the Greek*, New York: Simon and Schuster, 1952, p. 273.

2. J. Krishnamurti, *Krishnamurti's Notebook*, San Francisco: Harper Collins, 1976, p. 40.

Chapter Seven

ACCEPTING HARDSHIPS
AS THE PATHWAY TO PEACE

In an astonishing passage of Scripture, Saint Paul writes that "the message about the cross is foolishness to those who are perishing, but to us who are being saved it is the power of God" (1 Corinthians 1:18). Recalling our reflections in chapter 6 on eternal life, we now note the connection between the experience of eternal life and the cross of Jesus Christ.

The cross is perhaps one of the most misunderstood of all Christian teachings. While it is the symbol of our faith, many interpret it to mean that we should take upon ourselves the suffering of others. This seldom does much good in the long run, for it adds to the burdens of the one who does it, and deprives the other person of lessons to be learned. Another interpretation is that Jesus died to save us from our sins, and therefore we don't have to do anything to obtain the salvation he won for us. This line of thinking will lead us into irresponsibility. The true wisdom of the cross is much more profound, revealing something essential about the meaning of human suffering.

TWO KINDS OF SUFFERING

Everyone suffers from a wide variety of causes. In addition, there are different types of suffering, which we might call physical, emotional, and mental.

Physical suffering includes sickness, childbirth, injuries to the body, and other forms of bodily suffering. Fear, shame, anger, and disappointment are examples of emotional suffering. Mental suffering is confusion and ignorance. These three levels of suffering almost always coexist. Physical illness can produce emotional and mental suffering—for example, sadness and confusion—even though the physical level is most affected. Sadness can create mental and physical suffering—for example, confusion and physical sickness. Whenever there is pain of any kind, it is natural for the mind (the mental level) to become involved in the effort to get rid of the cause and the experience of the pain. We view our pain as a problem that has to be solved somehow so that we can be free of it. There is nothing wrong with this, of course; most of the discoveries of modern medicine have come from such intellectual efforts.

Another problem arises, however, when we interpret our pain in judgmental terms. Then we say that it is wrong or terrible to have this pain, and we conclude that we cannot know happiness unless the pain is gone. Whenever we do this, even to the slightest degree, we fall into the experience of linear time and we create time stress. We reject the experience of the Now as inadequate and place happiness in some future time when we assume better conditions for us will exist. Since eternal life is nothing but living fully in the Now, we cannot know eternal life when we reject the Now.

The rejection of inevitable pain is the root of unredemptive suffering and all forms of neurosis. It is unredemptive because we do not grow from it but become worse. It is suffering borne with impatience and anxiety. Many times, people also try to cope by using alcohol, drugs, and other addictive fixes to get out of their pain. This, too, is unredemptive, and it might even cause pain for other people, setting them going in a spiral of pain and judgment. Of course, the strategy that most people take to deal with pain is to try to change the outside world so that the cause of their pain is eliminated. Thus do we try to control people and circumstances beyond our control, contributing more pain and frustration to our lives and the lives of others (not to mention contributing to the destruction of the planet). In the end, unredemptive suffering leads to depression, hopelessness, and despair. We feel trapped, unable to change the world, other people, or ourselves enough to be free from pain. Since we believe that happiness is incompatible with suffering, we give up on ever experiencing happiness.

The other kind of suffering is redemptive. We can actually grow in many ways as we learn to walk with our pains. How might we do this? That's where the lesson of the cross comes in.

THE WISDOM OF THE CROSS

When Saint Paul tells us that the cross is the wisdom of God, he does not mean to say that suffering is a good thing, of course. Jesus worked many healings to help people become free from pain, and, like Jesus, we should do whatever we can to help others without creating unhealthy dependencies. What then could Saint Paul have been talking about?

For Saint Paul and the early Christians, there was no separating the crucifixion from the Resurrection of Jesus. It was the Resurrection that established Jesus as the Anointed of God and not simply one among many spiritually enlightened human beings who have walked the earth. To experience the energy of his risen life was, for them, the great gift that raised human consciousness to the level of eternal life. This gift became accessible to the human race because the Son of God took on human flesh and became one of us. So completely did he take on the human condition that he suffered the fate of a criminal and died as all people do. Thus did the life of God become directly present in the human species, raising us to a new level of being that far exceeded our previous state.

The cross as the wisdom of God is contrasted by Saint Paul with human wisdom, philosophy, and miraculous signs:

> Jews demand signs and Greeks desire wisdom, but we proclaim Christ crucified, a stumbling block to Jews and foolishness to Gentiles, but to those who are the called, both Jews and Greeks, Christ the power of God and the wisdom of God. For God's foolishness is wiser than human wisdom, and God's weakness is stronger than human strength (1 Corinthians 1:22-25).

God's power works through human weakness. What appears to be failure in human terms—the crucifixion—turns out to be victory! We don't need to be smart, beautiful, rich, or popular to know eternal life. What a relief! Because of Christ's crucifixion and resurrection, we see that what the world counts as gain means very little and what the world counts as nothing is very dear to God.

Saint Paul's conclusion from all of this is to ask "Who will separate us from the love of Christ? Will hardship, or distress, or persecution, or famine, or nakedness, or peril, or sword?" (Romans 8:35). In other words, suffering need not be an obstacle to eternal life; indeed, it might be a means by which we come to more deeply recognize the all-pervasive power of God's love.

THE WAY OF THE CROSS

The question for us, then, is not "Will we suffer?" but "How do we go about suffering?" Unredemptive suffering is one possibility, as we have already noted. But redemptive suffering—the way of the cross—is another possibility that we may choose to embrace.

Practically speaking, what would this entail? Consider the following:

- accept the inevitable pains that come your way without passing negative judgment on yourself or on the cause of your pain
- do what you can do to alleviate your pain without resorting to addictive fixes, which simply distort your mood or block the experience of the pain
- avoid making other people suffer because you are uncomfortable
- forgive those who have contributed to your pain
- do not overly identify with your pain because the real self is not the thoughts, feelings, or body that experience pain

This last point is most important. *The spiritual dimension of awareness knows no pain, and we experience eternal life in the spiritual dimension.* Pain is nothing but disharmony among the physical, emotional, and mental levels, and this turmoil is further agitated by judgmental thoughts and identification with pain. By identification, I mean such statements as "I am depressed," or "I'm frightened." The phrase "I am" is a statement of being; whatever we add to "I am" is an identification. So if I say "I am depressed," I identify myself with my depressed feelings and define myself in terms of them. This only increases my experience of gloom and cuts me off from the higher sources of wisdom and guidance available to me through the spiritual level of my being. The true self, on the other hand, *contains* the emotional level, but it also goes far beyond. Of the true self, all that can be said is "I am." To the extent that you can walk with your pain while awake to your true self, you will actually contribute to reducing pain.

None of this is to suggest that pain is an illusion, of course. It is real! Furthermore, it is important. Pain is the means by which we become aware of the disharmony in the different levels of our being. To ignore pain or to simply want it to disappear without correcting the disharmony is as silly as ignoring a warning light on an automobile or putting a piece of tape over the light so we won't notice it anymore. Correcting the disharmony is impossible if we do not first notice it and acknowledge what is happening. Next we must work to understand the cause of the disharmony and then eliminate it within ourselves. All of this must be done without self-judgment, or else disharmony will increase.

The best way to accept hardships, then, is to simply be aware of them with a nonjudgmental attitude. We say "There is sadness within me today" instead of "I am very sad today." As the Serenity Prayer notes, this simple act of acceptance is itself the pathway to peace; more healing will come from this acceptance than from any corrective disciplines we might undertake. Acceptance is the most effective means by which disharmony is quieted, and it is the key to opening ourselves to the wisdom revealed in each moment. Acting in union with the wisdom revealed by the Spirit within will eventually restore harmony.

For most people, the hardest part is this acceptance. They fear that if they really allow their pain to emerge, they won't be able to handle it. Therefore, they not only have pain, but in addition they are *fearful* of their pain. This, too, contributes to unredemptive suffering. What most find, however, is that this fear of pain is actually worse than the pain itself. By accepting pain and continuing to live attentively in the Now, we discover that we can handle whatever comes up. This brings freedom from the fear of pain—an enormous relief.

All of this goes against the conventional wisdom of the world. Those who decide to pick up their crosses and follow in the footsteps of Christ are truly countercultural people. They're also happier and more authentic people, which is far more important.

Eternal life—union with God—need not be lost because of pain. This is the wisdom of the cross. Those who accept it will find peace.

∽

Reflection and Practice

∼ How do you try to avoid inevitable pain? What consequences do you pay for this?

∼ What are the primary crosses you are carrying at this time in your life?

∼ What lessons are your crosses offering you?

∼ Make an effort to dis-identify with your pains. When noticing them, say "I feel (type of pain)" rather than "I am (type of pain)." Look upon them with love and acceptance as teachers who bring you important lessons.

Chapter Eight

TAKING, AS HE DID, THIS SINFUL WORLD AS IT IS, NOT AS I WOULD HAVE IT

THE WORLD IS a far from perfect place to live. Everyone knows this. The news media keep us well informed about all that is wrong with things, and goodness knows there is much to report. Political turmoil, economic instability, pollution, and violent crime are almost always in the headlines.

People respond to such dour information in many ways. Perhaps the most common is to become callous to it all. We've heard so much bad news through the years that, after a while, nothing surprises us any longer. We see graphic reports of casualties of earthquakes, floods, plane crashes, plagues, and warfare, and it does not phase us. "That's really too bad, but I'm afraid that's life," we might respond, with little emotional concern. We've become numb to the pain of the world because it seems so commonplace.

For many, the experience of life as a troublesome affair hits a lot closer to home. Those who grow up in unhealthy families have experienced firsthand the meaning of rejection or even abuse. They may doubt the reality of goodness, care, and love. Wounded at all levels of their being, they are frequently cynical about life's meaning. As someone once wrote, "Life is a banquet, but most people are starving to death."

THEOLOGY AND EVIL

This part of the Serenity Prayer acknowledges the reality of evil and proposes an attitude with which to face it. No philosophy or theology can stand the test of time if it fails to account for the reality of pain and misery. Managing to salvage a sense of the meaning of life in the face of such negativity is most difficult, for evil seems to negate the supremacy of God's power and goodness. As many people have said many times, evil suggests that God is all-good but not all-powerful, or else it suggests that God is all-powerful but not all-good.

Christian theologians have grappled with this problem for centuries, and they always seem to come to similar conclusions. Evil, they tell us, is first and foremost a mystery. We do not fully understand everything about the existence of evil and its role in God's plan for the universe. At the same time, theologians affirm that everything created by God is good; God does not make anything to be evil. Evil, then, is a perversion of something that was once good but has become disordered or spoiled. The only creatures who can truly be evil are spiritual beings, for only they can choose to reject the good. We might call a tornado evil, but it is really not good or bad; it's just a tornado and it cannot be otherwise. This is not the case with spiritual beings like angels and humans, who are conscious of their intelligence and freedom. Depending on how we use these gifts, we can be good or evil. In the case of an angel, the consequences are absolute. Because the angel knows fully what it is doing, its choices manifest full acceptance or rejection of God's will. Not so with human beings, who are somewhat good and somewhat evil, for we usually do not fully comprehend the implications of our decisions.

But what about God and evil? If God creates a being who can become evil, then doesn't evil exist as a possibility within God? Can't God do something to stop evil?

Christian theologians respond by noting that since evil is not really some-*thing* but is the perversion of the good, evil is not created by God. The only thing God could do to stop evil in its tracks would be to withdraw the gift of freedom that God has given to those creatures who have become evil. God could certainly do this, but what would be left would be a robotic, instinctual creature and not a spiritual one.

What is profound is that in creating us free—even free to do evil—God has chosen to allow us and all of creation to experience the consequences of our use and misuse of freedom. It is as though, in creating us free, God has accepted certain limitations in God's response to our use of freedom. God can certainly prevent us from doing wrong, but to do so would violate the very freedom to do wrong (and to do right) that God has given us in the first place. What God creates is a being who is good and free, but the evil built up through centuries of wrong-choosing infects us with a conditioning that biases many of our choices toward evil. As the Scriptures emphasize again and again, this situation causes enormous grief for God, and yet God refuses to withdraw the precious gift of freedom. What can God do, however, besides watch us bring ourselves to ruin? Surely God's heart must be moved to do something about this—something that does not annihilate the gift of freedom. That's where Christ comes in.

CHRIST AND EVIL

God knows very well the sad predicament in which the human race finds itself—infected by evil and unable to break completely free of it. All world religions deal with this issue in various ways. All emphasize the importance of morality and detachment from addictive pursuits, and all promise an experience of some kind of liberation. This is true in Christianity as well, with one profound difference. Christianity speaks not only of a path of liberation from evil (and the recovery of true freedom and goodness) but also of a *new human nature* in which this can be accomplished. God saw that human nature was irreparably wounded by sin, and so God created a new human being—Jesus Christ—who was at once both human and divine. Through his death, resurrection, and ascension, Christ became immediately present to all who live, making available to us the wisdom and power to overcome evil. In responding to evil in this manner, God did not destroy the human nature already created. Its freedom and intelligence remain, and it is to these human qualities that the Church appeals when inviting people to faith. For although Christ is present to all, it is through faith that we fully and consciously enter into his life and partake in his Spirit. This is the way God has worked in the Judeo-Christian tradition to respond to the problem of evil.

EVIL AND SPIRITUALITY

Spirituality puts into practice the truths affirmed by theology. What the Christian experiences is precisely what theology affirms: faith in Christ does indeed give us more power to do good and resist evil. However, evil presents many difficult problems for spiritual practice. Even as we are being healed by Christ's power, the wounding of our nature by sin nonetheless persists. We must learn to go to Christ who accepts us just as we are, with all our weaknesses and evil inclinations; then he begins to nudge us in the direction of greater health and harmony.

We must learn to perceive these movements of his Spirit and to respond. If we resist him, he allows us to live with our consequences. This seems to be the way things go—responding, falling, getting up, going again, falling, and so on—until we learn how to walk with him and live more fully the new life he came to give us. To do this, we will need to avail ourselves of many resources. Scripture, Church teaching, the sacraments, prayer, and the support of other Christians are indispensable. All these gifts enable us to abide more fully in the Christ life.

But what about that evil world out there? Shouldn't we do something to clean it all up—especially once we come to know the reality of Christ?

Indeed, we should, but there are some ways that work better than others. Enthusiastic idealism, for example, is one response we see in many, especially recent converts. They know how good and right Christ has been for them, and they want everyone to know the same. They preach about him whenever they can, and they would have every secular institution explicitly grounded in Christ. Such enthusiasm has its place, but it seldom endures and is often counterproductive. We live in a pluralistic society that will never (at least in this age) base itself fully on gospel principles.

Nevertheless, as the Scriptures and documents of Vatican II affirm, Christians have a duty to bring the gospel into the world and to become a leavening through which goodness will grow. The way we do this is the same way our Master did—by loving the world into goodness. That's where the advice given in this line of the Serenity Prayer comes in: "Taking, as He did, this sinful world as it is, not as I would have it."

Jesus Christ surely knew that the world was sinful—that certain social structures had become supports for evil rather than good and that religious authorities were misusing their influence, among many other evils. He also knew that it would do little good to try to improve society if people's hearts were not changed. He confronted evil—including the evil of certain social structures—whenever he could, but he focused more on helping people to change their lives. "Taking this sinful world as it is" meant, for him, accepting this as the reality in which he was sent to love. He knew very well the kind of kingdom that existed in heaven, and he longed for it to become manifest on earth (the world as he "would have it"). But he realized that the way to get from the sinful reality to the kingdom fully manifest begins with *unconditional love for what is*. He found us sinful, and he loved us in this condition, enabling us to become more good and loving ourselves.

We are called to do the same. If we grew up in a troubled family, we can accept and love our family members just as they are. Perhaps, in time, they will change. If we work in an institution where there are unjust laws and practices, we can love the people who govern there and in time challenge them to change this situation. If we are persecuted by someone, we can resist returning insult for injury and instead love this person as best we can.

Of course, the first place to start is with ourselves.

Do we love and accept ourselves just as we are? We have already said something about this in earlier chapters, but we cannot ever say we are done with this one. The infection of sin in our souls urges us to neglect ourselves, sometimes even in the name of Christian love. For example, when we make loving another person more important than loving and accepting ourselves, we run the risk of codependency. This line of the Serenity Prayer needs to be applied to self as well as to others and institutions. "Taking, as He did, this sinful person just as I am and not as I would have myself" means that we cannot put off opening ourselves to God's love until such time as we are good, or moral, or perfect (whatever that might mean). The person God loves is this good creature who has been infected by sin. God loves this person *now*, in this moment. No need to wait for it to happen; it's already here. To open ourselves to it is to taste eternal life.

~

Reflection and Practice

~ Examine the conditions for love and acceptance you have placed on yourself, other people, and the world. For example:

Self: I could love myself more if only I would

- lose 20 pounds
- stop smoking

~ After you have gotten in touch with this conditional aspect of your love, make an affirmation of faith:

"God loves me totally even with my extra weight and even if I smoke cigarettes."

~ Repeat this affirmation slowly and prayerfully, allowing yourself to feel the truth of the statement. If you feel moved to express gratitude, remorse, or some other emotion to God, go ahead and do so. Do this affirmation each day and continue until you feel that you experience God's unconditional love in this part of your life.

~ Continue with your spouse, children, job, relatives, government, and any other important people and institutions in your life. Begin with noting the conditionality of your love, and follow with an affirmation that expresses God's unconditional love.

~ Such affirmations do not condone the faults you are aware of but bring you in touch with the love and acceptance through which you can perhaps eventually change them.

Chapter Nine

TRUSTING THAT HE WILL MAKE ALL THINGS RIGHT

DEVELOPMENTAL PSYCHOLOGISTS tell us that the issue of trust in the basic goodness of life is one of the first issues we deal with after birth. Depending on how we are treated by our parents and other caretakers, we develop deep inner convictions about the trustworthiness of life. If all goes well, we carry with us forever this basic sense that life is okay—even if we are abused later in life. If we don't receive the kind of early nurturing we need—lots of touching and hugging—we are left with fear and anxiety toward other people and life in general. In response to this fear, we develop defenses and adopt an attitude of taking control over the situation in which we find ourselves. Because no one is raised in an environment of perfect love, we all possess this attitude of defensiveness and distrust to some degree.

In many ways, the spiritual life offers us an opportunity to start over with our development. Our wounds are many and they are deep, but the Holy Spirit who dwells within can touch us in our deepest depths. If we are practicing the attitudes and disciplines recommended in the Serenity Prayer thus far, we will find ourselves opening more and more to the reality and guidance of the Spirit. The issue that now faces us is that of trust in God. God can touch us very deeply, but do we want to continue to open ourselves to God? Do we want our development to unfold henceforth under the direction of the Spirit? If so, where will we be led?

MAKING ALL THINGS RIGHT

The Serenity Prayer gives a response to these questions: God will lead us in such a manner that all will be right with our lives. We are back to the affirmation made in chapter 1: in God's reign, all shall be well. But what does this mean? After all, we naturally wonder about the rewards for investing ourselves in something. We would never sign on to a financial program, for example, without a general idea of what we might get out of it. Why not so with God?

In reading through the gospels, we will find much to help us understand the meaning of "making all things right." We learn that there are no guarantees of monetary wealth, worldly popularity, or even the approval of our family. If we have been trusting in these for our happiness and security, we will be disappointed to know that following Christ might bring us the complete opposite. The only absolute guarantee we have is that nothing can separate us from the love of Christ. Even if we are worried or persecuted, starving or naked, threatened or even attacked, Christ will always be there for us with his love (see Romans 8:35). That is all. The revelation of this truth is what Christ brought us through his life, death, and resurrection. God is with us, loving us in this very moment with no strings attached. All shall be well for those who believe in and act upon this great good news!

In an earlier book, I listed some of the promises of God to those who follow Christ:

1. Those who give to the poor will be rewarded (Matthew 6:4).
2. God hears our prayers and knows our needs (Matthew 6:59).
3. Those who ask, search, and knock on the doors of life for grace will receive it (Matthew 7:7-11).
4. God will give the Holy Spirit to those who ask (Luke 11:9-13).
5. Living according to Christ's way will bring stability into life (Matthew 7:27).
6. Those who follow Christ will find rest for their souls (Matthew 18:19-20).
7. Christ will be present when two or more gather in his name (Matthew 18:19-20).
8. Christians will receive repayment many times over in this life for leaving the past behind and following Jesus (Luke 18:28-30).
9. Those who believe in Jesus will do the same works that he did (John 14:12).
10. Jesus will give to his followers a peace that surpasses understanding (John 14:27).
11. If we remain in Christ, we may ask whatever we want and we will get it (John 15:7).
12. Living the Christian life will bring us joy (John 16:24).[1]

This gives us an idea of what God making all things right can mean for us. Many of these promises have to do with healing, wholeness, peace, and joy. John 10:10 sums it up best when Christ says: "I came that they may have life, and have it abundantly."

TRUSTING IN GOD

How easy it is to read (or even to preach or write) about God making all things right, but how difficult to base our lives on this truth! We have been so conditioned in anxiety that the ideal of completely entrusting our lives to the care of God seems unattainable.

Maybe we need to modify this expectation, however. Maybe completely trusting in God is just not possible right now. Maybe all that we can expect is to trust as much as we can, knowing that we can always trust more. This is more attainable, and it is, at any rate, all that we can do! But how would this work?

Trust is reliance on the character, ability, strength, or truth of someone. Trust is different from love. Love is a gift, but trust must be earned. Parents know very well that it is possible to love a child while not necessarily trusting that child with regard to a certain issue. If my daughter breaks her curfew, I will still love her, but I won't rely as much on the truth of her word until she begins to consistently demonstrate fidelity to the curfew. She must earn my trust, but she will always have my love.

Why should it not be the same in our relationship with God? We can only trust God to the degree that we believe we can depend on the character, ability, strength, and truth of God. We cannot give absolute and total trust right away, and I'm sure God knows this very well. It might sound irreverent to say it, but God realizes that our trust must be earned, and God is willing to enter into relationship with us under these circumstances. What God wants, however, is a chance to prove trustworthiness. How would we give God this chance?

It is here that the issue of risk comes in. I cannot learn to trust my daughter with keeping a curfew unless I give her a chance to actually do it. If she comes through, then I trust her more and become willing to take other risks with her. Likewise, we must learn to take risks with God as well. If we don't, then we're holding on to control and keeping God on a leash. And so we must venture a risk in some area of our lives, taking God up on God's word and acting as if God were speaking truth on this issue.

TAKING A RISK WITH GOD

How would you take a risk with God?

There are a number of ways to do this. First, you might consider some of the promises from Scripture listed above. Most of them are pretty general, and all are hard to measure. But let's suppose you decide to take Christ up on asking, seeking, and knocking in prayer. Perhaps you have a petition you want to pray about; or, even better, you might have a desire to grow closer to Christ through prayer. Taking a risk, here, would require that you actually take the time to pray—and regularly! If you are not already spending time each day in prayer, you would have to find it, which means that you would have to give up something else in order to pray. All risks require sacrifice; otherwise they are not really risks.

Sometimes your risk-taking might not be so explicitly oriented toward God as in the above example. For example, you might give up a bad habit like smoking or eating junk food and begin doing something good for your health instead. As you experience the positive consequences for doing so, you learn to trust more in the goodness of life and the reality of living more fully. This cannot help but increase your trust in the Creator who makes such growth possible.

In closing, I offer this marvelous poem (authorship unknown). It captures very nicely the importance of risk-taking, and I believe its relevance to the spiritual life will become obvious:

Risk

To laugh is to risk appearing the fool.
To weep is to risk appearing sentimental.
To reach out for another is to risk involvement.
To expose your feelings is to risk exposing your
　　true self.
To place your ideas, your dreams before the
　　crowd
is to risk their loss.
To love is to risk not being loved in return.
To live is to risk dying.
To hope is to risk despair.
To try is to risk failure.
But risks must be taken because the greatest
　　hazard
is to risk nothing.
Those who risk nothing
do nothing,
have nothing
and are nothing.
They may avoid suffering and sorrow,
but they simply cannot learn, feel, change, grow,
　　love, live.
Chained by their own fears, they are slaves;
They have forfeited freedom.
Only a person who risks is free.[2]

Reflection and Practice

~ What makes it difficult for you to trust in God?

~ When confronted with a situation in which you are called to take a risk, pray "Jesus, I trust in you," then do what you are called to do, knowing that Christ is with you.

---

1. Philip St. Romain, *Becoming a New Person: Twelve Steps to Christian Growth*, Liguori, MO: Liguori Publications, 1984, p.11.
2. Author unknown, "Risk," [http://www.montego.com/~ed2000pl/p0000095.htm].

Chapter Ten

IF I SURRENDER
TO HIS WILL

THE IDEA OF surrendering to God's will is rife with mis-understandings. Indeed, it is sobering to note that the phrase *doing God's will* is seldom used in Scripture. This is not the common language of the New Testament but of a later time in Church history when the school of theology called *scholasticism* was predominant. This theological approach ruled Catholic thinking from the thirteenth century through the middle of the twentieth century, and it made a strong impact on Protestantism as well. It was based on the philosophy of Aristotle, especially as interpreted by Saint Thomas Aquinas in the light of divine revelation. We find hardly a trace of scholastic thinking in most books on theology and spirituality today. And yet we are left with many scholastic concepts, not the least of which is the notion of God's will.

To demonstrate how poorly our modern understanding of God's will connects with the scholastic understanding, I will share a true story about a friend of mine named Troy. He was raised in the Catholic Church and was a faithful Catholic. He attended Church regularly, married in the Church, had his three children baptized, and belonged to the Knights of Columbus. At the age of thirty-two, he attended a Cursillo retreat and experienced his faith coming alive in a new way. He followed this up with involvement in the Catholic charismatic renewal, where he experienced anew the reality of the Holy Spirit. Within a few weeks, Troy had gone from being a "normal Catholic" to being a man totally on fire for the gospel. All he wanted to do was pray, read Scripture, go to prayer meetings, and talk to people about Jesus. He lost interest in his work, and his wife's tepid faith (compared to his, that is) bothered him enormously. It wasn't long before he began to question what was God's will for him, going so far as to wonder if God wanted him to leave his lukewarm wife, get an annulment, and begin studying for the priesthood. He began second-guessing if his initial decision to marry had gone against God's will, and whether the career he had studied for was God's will for him. In short, Troy was very confused, and his ideas about God's will were at the root of his problems.

I'm happy to report that Troy eventually worked his way through all these issues. Counseling with a priest friend and with a spiritual director helped him to recognize that God had been with him all along, even before his faith was more awakened. He came to see that loving his wife and caring for his children were God's will for him, as was his choice of a career. His newfound love for ministry needed attention, however, and so he began to volunteer his services more for liturgy and retreat work. Several years later, Troy entered the diaconate program for his diocese and was recently ordained as a permanent deacon.

IMAGES OF GOD'S WILL

When the term *God's will* is mentioned, what comes to mind? For many, there is a heaviness about the concept, almost as though God's will is a burden added to already difficult lives. I might think of God's will as a *doing* kind of thing: God wants me to do something, and I have to find out what it is so I can do it and please God. This is similar to the divine playwright image: God has a role for me to play in life, and I must discover it so I can fulfill God's plan for me. In these two images, God's will is perceived as a mandate of some kind that God already knows but that I have to discover. If, in addition, I was raised in a religious culture where ministers were thought to be closer to God than ordinary folks, I could easily conclude that the best way to follow God's will is to become a minister of some kind. This is the image that was responsible for Troy's confusion. Because he had come to feel closer to God, he believed that this must signify a call to ministry.

None of these images are true to what the scholastic theologians have in mind when they refer to God's will, however. Will, for them, is a characteristic of a spiritual being, as is intelligence. To say that God is the Supreme Being means that God has Supreme Intelligence and Will. God's Supreme Intelligence is discussed in terms of God's Omniscience—God knows everything that can and will happen or even might happen. God's Omnipotence—that God is all-powerful—was the supreme quality of God's Will. God as all-powerful and all-knowing: what do these images do for you?

Having acknowledged these qualities of God, the scholastics go on to describe how lesser spiritual beings like humans and angels could come to union with God. They note that since God is all-knowing and the breadth of God's knowledge is infinite, then it is impossible for a lesser spirit to be one with God at the level of knowledge. God's ways are not our ways, and

God's thoughts are as high above ours as the heavens are above the earth, noted Isaiah the prophet (see Isaiah 55:8-9). We can know lots of theology and Scripture, but this knowledge does not constitute a very profound type of union with God.

Since the scholastics consider union with God through knowledge impossible, we might think that union through will is even more difficult, for God's power is certainly infinite, and our own is not. That's where the great surprise comes in, however. God's power is indeed infinite, but it is not the power of brute force. God's power, or manner of influencing creation, has been revealed as pure Love. To say that God is all-powerful is to acknowledge that God is all-loving. This is revealed most clearly in the crucifixion of Jesus, in which he rejects the use of legions of angels to overcome his foes. Instead, he proceeds lovingly to the end, and the all-powerful energy of Love raises him up on the third day to be the Lord of Love forever.

What the scholastics concluded from this is that while it is impossible to attain union with God through knowledge, it is possible to be fully united with God through love. Just as two burning candles can be brought together to form one flame, so can the will of God and a human being come together to form one great love. In this love, the human is still human and God is still God, but the two are not-separate. The light that burns belongs to both, and this is the light the world needs to see.

SURRENDERING TO GOD'S WILL

Now that we understand the meaning of the term *God's will*, we can better carry out what is proposed in this line of the Serenity Prayer. In the previous chapter, we noted that God would make all things right, and now we affirm that this will indeed be the case if we surrender to God's will. Practically speaking, this means that we choose love itself as our greatest priority in life. We all live by values, and we give a different priority to each of our values. Choosing love as the most important of our values means that we place it above the will to pleasure, wealth, power, or any other pursuit. When we need to make a decision, we consider the practical aspects of the situation, but we pay most attention to the requirements of love in that situation.

Of course, we might be suffering from dysfunctional beliefs about love itself, just as we do about God's will. That's why it's important to read Scripture, study Church teaching, and, most importantly, get to know Jesus Christ. We really do suffer from crazy, codependent ideas about love, and Christ can help us understand the true meaning of love. Let's take a few common examples of healthy and unhealthy images of love.

Consider, for example, the connection between God's love and your happiness. Sometimes people think that if they truly love as Christ loved, they should have no thought of their own happiness, but only of others'. When given an opportunity for greater happiness, they almost automatically reject the offer, thinking they are doing a very spiritual thing. Can you imagine how this must make God feel? Put yourself in God's place. There you are, loving someone fully, hoping that your love will enable them to experience the fullness of life, and they choose unhappiness instead! God wills our happiness: this we must never forget. (We will reflect more on this in our next chapter.) If our inner light and God's shine as one, we will accept happiness as a gift from God and not deny ourselves the blessings of life.

Let's try another one—God's love and your unique-ness. Many people think that God's will is that they become someone different from the person they already are. This is true, of course, if we're talking about our bad habits or our inclinations to sin. Defects of charac-ter must go, but it would be wrong to say that these defects define who we are. God made each one of us unique; such was God's intention. Now can you imag-ine how it must make God feel when, in the name of religion or God's will, we deny our uniqueness and try to imitate someone else? Imitating another—a saint or even Christ himself—is generally psychologically dam-aging, unless we are talking about imitating them in virtue. We cannot and should not try to do what an-other person did unless it is an authentic expression of our own will to love.

What is important is to do God's will as yourself—not someone else—and to find your happiness in doing so. This is the yoke that Jesus talks about in Matthew 11:29-30: "Take my yoke upon you, and learn from me," he says, "for I am gentle and humble in heart, and you will find rest for your souls. For my yoke is easy, and my burden is light." The yoke of God's total love for you is what enables you to accept your uniqueness and your happiness as God's great gift to you.

DISCERNING GOD'S WILL

A healthy understanding of God's will is most criti-cal in the area of discernment. God's will is love, and God wills our uniqueness and happiness. However, this does not invalidate the possibility that, in certain cir-cumstances, God is calling us to do a certain kind of work. There is a distinction between God's general will for us and God's specific will for an individual in a situation. We have reflected briefly on God's general will, and it must be the context in which we try to discern God's specific will for us. Should we marry or not, pursue this career or that one, change jobs, move to another city? Often in life, we find ourselves facing these kinds of questions. How do we make decisions about them? What criteria do we use? How can we tell if God is calling us to one path instead of another?

The first thing we can say with confidence is that true discernment is not about whether to do wrong or to do good. Because God's will is love, it is never God's will that we sin. When we speak of discernment, we are talking about choosing among options that are not sinful but good. Is it possible, however, that one option is better than the other because of what an individual needs at this time in life to grow in God's will?

These are the issues that spiritual direction deals with. They can be tricky, and it would be impossible to deal with them exhaustively in this small space. Generally, it takes time to discern an important issue, and it is best to do so in dialogue with a spiritual director or other people attuned to God's ways. There are almost never any great magical signs—no tablets of stone on which we find our answers. Through the process of weighing alternatives, dialoguing with others, and praying about things, one particular option begins to feel right. I know that doesn't sound like much to go on, but it really is the best guide to making a good decision. If we don't come to this sense of an inner conviction, we just use our reason to make what seems to be a good choice, knowing that God will go with us no matter what we choose. (This is also true even if we happen to make poor, impulsive decisions, only we will probably pay negative consequences for these.)

No one—not even a saint or a spiritual director— can tell you what God's will is for you. If someone tries to do this, don't listen to them. Discerning God's will is a matter of the heart and not a matter of obedience to an external authority. Surrendering to God's will is about awakening to the reality of one's own inner authority, which most people have lost. This inner authority is the place within where our spirit and God's Spirit agree on a certain course of action. To invalidate this authority is a very serious matter; when it is lost, so is one's experience of union with God. When we are true to this authority, however, we realize the true meaning of this part of the Serenity Prayer: we trust that God will make all things right, if we surrender to God's will.

Reflection and Practice

~ What has your image of doing God's will been like? How has the discussion in this chapter influenced your understanding of the meaning of the term *God's will*?

~ How can you better surrender your will to the care of God?

~ How do you give away your inner authority to others?

~ What kinds of decisions do you need to struggle with to discern God's will?

Chapter Eleven

THAT I MAY BE
REASONABLY HAPPY IN THIS LIFE

IN MANY WAYS, everything written in earlier chapters about serenity also applies to happiness. However, serenity is a state of being that ensues from union with God, while happiness comes from the fulfillment of desire. There's obviously a relationship between these two, but there are also differences. One person might experience serenity, for example, without a great deal of happiness, and another might taste deeply of happiness without knowing the peace that surpasses understanding. Desire is what makes the difference between the two types of experiences. Some people may abide in serenity without experiencing much desire, in which case the experience of happiness will be minimal. Others, as we know, abide in desire without much serenity, and taste happiness when their desires are fulfilled. The problem is that if someone has the wrong kinds of desires, then happiness is fleeting and unhappiness follows in its wake.

HAPPINESS AND DESIRE

Let's reflect more deeply on the experience of desire and how it works. All the world religions have been concerned with the problem of desire. In Buddhism, for example, desire is named as the root cause of unhappiness. The purpose of the Eightfold Path of Buddhism is to extinguish desire and, with it, the experience of unhappiness (or sorrow, as the Buddhists put it). The wisdom here is flawless: if a person desires nothing, then that person can never be disappointed, hurt, or anxious. Many have come to peace and fulfillment following this path. It would be mistaken to conclude that Buddhist detachment negates care and concern for the welfare of others. Compassion is, for Buddhists, a sure sign of walking the path of freedom. Highly advanced mystics (Bodhisattvas) also renounce the final stages of enlightenment until every sentient being has been enlightened, and they vow to work for this end until death.

Like Buddhism, Christianity emphasizes detachment from the things of this world, which can only disappoint us if and when we lose them. Nothing created is permanent, and so to center our happiness on anyone or anything is a setup for unhappiness. On this point, we are one with Buddhists. There is a positive aspect to desire in Christianity, however, that is not present in Buddhism. Buddhism is nontheistic (which is different from atheistic: Buddhists do not deny the existence of God as atheists do; they just don't speak of God). Christianity is theistic (that is, we believe in God). Because Christians believe that all God created is good, we view desire not as something to be extinguished but as a good and holy characteristic of our creatureliness. We desire because we have needs, and desire is intended to move us to fulfill our needs.

The problem is that our desires have become multiplied and disordered because of sin. So often we do not seek what will fulfill our true needs. Instead, we pursue what will temporarily alleviate the experience of anxiety and shame resulting from our loss of full union with

God. We turn to food, relationships, television, sex, work, and other involvements, not so much for the nourishment they can bring to our lives but for the escape they provide. Then we cling to them as though they are our own. We try to control them so that they will always be there when we need them.

Without a doubt, we need to make a break with disordered desires and addictions. The Twelve-Step process used in recovery groups has been a gift to the people of this century to help them make this break. I believe Buddhism can also teach us much about growing in inner freedom through its Four Noble Truths. Those who use these approaches in the context of Christian spirituality will need to emphasize the positive aspect of desire as well as the negative or detachment dimension. By this I mean that, while disengaging the energy of desire from its harmful preoccupations, we need to reorient desire to its true purpose. And what might that purpose be? As the old catechisms put it, our purpose is to know, love, and serve God.

CHRISTIANITY AND DESIRE

The resolution of the problem of desire in Christianity, then, is ultimately achieved by making our greatest desire the love of God. The first great commandment, Jesus tells us, is to love the Lord our God with all our heart, with all our soul, with all our mind, and with all our strength (Mark 12:30). If we cultivate this desire above all others, then we will come to know union with God, and we will come to know serenity. We will still experience other desires, of course. When we are hungry, we will desire food; when we are working, we will desire just pay.

In fact, loving God above all else allows us to desire more things than ever before. Do you want wealth? Go for it! Sex? Enjoy it as much as you and your spouse desire! Just so long as you love God above all else, you can pursue whatever desires you wish. The nonfulfillment of those lesser desires will not bring you great unhappiness. You might be disappointed when your desires are not fulfilled, but you can let go of these setbacks and move on with your life.

Of course, what usually happens is that when we love God above all else, our desires for people and things change in many ways. We begin to want whatever will help us live in union, and we begin to reject whatever takes us away from God. We might still experience temptation, but it doesn't have the power that it once held over us. We might still desire worldly things like wealth, but we hold this desire more loosely. If it comes to pass, fine; if not, then we already possess the pearl of great price, which is the love of God.

The second great commandment provides a complementary orientation for desire—to love our neighbor as ourselves (Mark 12:31). In addition, the Lord's Prayer urges us to pray "thy kingdom come, thy will be done, on earth as it is in heaven." We cannot simply rest in a state of serenity in which we experience all to be well in our own personal lives because we know God's love. The ultimate liberation of Christian desire happens when that desire reaches out to the earth as well as to heaven. The Lord's Prayer commands us to *long* for the coming of the kingdom and to pray for the "daily bread" that will enable us to *work* for its coming. Like the Buddhist mystic who longs for the liberation of all sentient creatures, the Christian longs for the coming of the reign of God in all levels of society. Each of us is called to do this in a unique way, and so there is no point in comparing ourselves to one another or to great social reformers like Dorothy Day and Mother Teresa. "How do you want me to build your kingdom, Lord?" This is the question that should direct our desires.

HAPPINESS AND CHRIST

The two great commandments and the Lord's Prayer give us a glimpse of the desires of Christ. Those who live as his disciples will find their own desires transformed as they grow closer to him. We will begin to want what he wants and therefore do what he does. This is the ideal, but it is one we can realize to some degree. Since happiness comes from the fulfillment of desire, we can experience happiness as Christ does if we desire as he desires.

This might sound strange to many, but it's right there in the gospels as one of the promises of Christ. In chapter 1 we noted that he promised us peace, not as the world gives but as he gives. Now we will reflect briefly on an amazing discourse of Christ from John 15:7-11:

> If you abide in me, and my words abide in you, ask for whatever you wish, and it will be done for you. My Father is glorified by this, that you bear much fruit and become my disciples. As the Father has loved me, so I have loved you; abide in my love. If you keep my commandments, you will abide in my love, just as I have kept my Father's commandments and abide in his love. I have said these things to you so that my joy may be in you, and that your joy may be complete.

By keeping the two great commandments, we remain in Christ by joining our desires with his. This, as we noted in our previous chapter, is how we attain union with God through love. What is remarkable about the present passage is that Jesus is encouraging those who have attained this union to "ask for whatever you wish," and he promises that "it will be done for you." He wants us to do this so that we will bear much fruit to the glory of God and so that our joy may be completed by his own joy. In other words, he wants to share his own happiness with us, and he wants to do so by giving us what we ask for. He delights in giving to us, just as a parent delights in giving a child something that will make the child happy.

What a positive message! How slow we are to take Christ at his word! Could it be that many of us aren't as happy as we would like to be because we aren't exercising our desire for happiness by asking for God's blessings? I suspect we disappoint God in this way just as much as we do through our sins. God wants to bless us with the joy of Christ. If that is what we desire, too, then we will not be disappointed.

~

Reflection and Practice

~ What are your predominant desires? How do they contribute to your experiences of happiness and unhappiness?

~ What do you want from God? How are you asking and seeking for this?

~ God wants to shower you with blessings. Do you believe this? Why or why not?

~ Use the affirmation "Bless me, Lord."

Chapter Twelve

AND SUPREMELY HAPPY
WITH HIM FOREVER

IT IS FITTING that this final phrase of the Serenity Prayer is an affirmation of hope. Traditionally, hope has been considered one of the three theological virtues, along with faith and love. In 1 Corinthians 13:13, Saint Paul states that "faith, hope, and love abide, these three; and the greatest of these is love." I do not doubt for one second that the experience of love is more meaningful than hope, but I wonder if such love can be sustained without hope. I rather doubt it.

What is hope? *The Catechism of the Catholic Church* (#2090) defines hope as the "confident expectation of divine blessing and the beatific vision of God; it is also the fear of offending God's love and of incurring punishment."[1] Hope is related to the spiritual desires and longings we discussed in the previous chapter, but hope has two very explicit orientations. First, it is a longing for the beatific vision, and second, it is a longing to avoid losing such a blessing. This chapter will deal with these two topics.

THE TRUE GOAL OF CHRISTIANITY

Any organization that forgets its primary goal is bound to fail. Can you imagine what would happen if, for example, the U.S. Postal Service forgot that its primary goal is to deliver mail and packages as quickly and inexpensively as possible? Suppose, instead, they began to act out of a different goal—like providing employment for people who need jobs. This might make a lot of their employees happy, but it won't necessarily serve the consumer very well. Suppose, again, that the goal of a teacher was to have the students' good opinion? The class might be fun to attend, but it is doubtful that anyone would learn very much.

Almost every company these days works out of a mission statement, which in turn provides a stimulus for setting objectives and goals. Many consultants to corporations are quick to point out that companies that attend to their true goals and priorities will succeed more often than those that get distracted by other concerns. Putting first things first is sound business practice, and it also works in the realm of relationships as well. A wife and husband who allow work, children, and other concerns to come between them will find their love diminished. Life is about making choices, and if one does not choose according to one's priorities, then the results are going to be disappointing.

What about the realm of religion and spirituality? Does it work the same way?

It surely does—at least it's supposed to. Jesus tells us to make God's kingdom and righteousness our first priority (see Matthew 6:33). The early fathers of the Church spoke about this in terms of divinization. This is a term seldom heard, but it is a powerful idea that remains as valid and inspiring now as then, for it describes what is really going on in the spiritual life.

Put simply, divinization is the process through which our human consciousness is transformed so that it is taken up into the consciousness of God. It's easy enough for us to know what our human consciousness is: it's our human way of knowing, feeling, desiring, remembering, and so on. It's easy, too, to acknowledge that this individual human consciousness of ours is not the same as God's. Whatever God's consciousness might be like (if, indeed, it is even appropriate to speak about God in this way), we know very well that we are not God—at least not the God that religion speaks about (all-powerful, all-knowing, all-good, and all-loving). And yet, amazingly, the true goal and promise of Christianity is that this very limited human consciousness of ours is becoming changed in many subtle ways through the grace of the Spirit so that we can enter more and more fully into the very life and consciousness of God.

The full realization of this is called the beatific vision. In a reflection on the beatific vision in his *Dictionary of Theology*, Karl Rahner observes that "in the beatific vision the reality of the mind as a knower is the being of God himself." The beatific vision is "a taking up into the source....It is only in the intuitive beatific vision that God's utter incomprehensibility is contemplated in itself with all its radicality."[2] Saint Paul seems to be saying something similar when he notes: "Now we see in a mirror, dimly, but then we will see face to face. Now I know only in part; then I will know fully, even as I have been fully known" (1 Corinthians 13:12).

This—and not floating around on clouds while playing a harp—is the heaven of Christianity. It is the full integration of the human into the divine, which enables us to know with God's knowing, to love with God's loving, and to rejoice in the supreme happiness that only God enjoys. It is a possibility won for us by Christ, who in his person joined together the human and divine modes of being, and now enables us to become as he is through the gift of his own Spirit. It is also a process at work in us that can be realized in the "reasonable happiness" we can experience in him during this life but which will be ultimately fulfilled after death.

HOPE AND HEAVEN

As the *Catechism* puts it, "Hope is the confident expectation of divine blessing and the beatific vision" (#2090).[3] I wonder sometimes how strong this hope is among Christians. Do we have our hearts set on the realization of heaven? I don't think we pay nearly as much attention to our true goal and priority as we should. If we ran our businesses like we run our spiritual lives, many of us would be bankrupt—which is precisely the spiritual situation in which millions find themselves.

A few misunderstandings prevail concerning the issue of hoping for heaven. The first is that our popular understanding of heaven falls far short of the true meaning of the beatific vision. The concept of heaven that most people entertain is extremely dull and unimaginative. As a young student recently observed, "I'm not sure I really want to go to heaven; it sounds like a very dull place." *The Far Side* cartoonist Gary Larson has a scene with a man in a robe sitting on a cloud with his harp and a bored look on his face, thinking that he wished he'd brought a magazine along. Something like this is what the young student had in mind. I might add that he had absolutely no doubt in his mind about his material goals. He wanted to make a lot of money, and he had a plan for doing it.

I can't say I blame the student much for his disinterest in heaven, because I think the Church has done a poor job in getting us excited about it. Granted that the topic is not an easy one to do justice to, still, we cannot expect people to grow in the virtue of hope if they never reflect on heaven, which is hope's truest and deepest orientation. We cannot expect the faithful to be able to face death with courage—never mind anticipation!—if they have little hope.

What happens when people have little hope in the future—their own or that of the world as a whole? Without a future to hope in and to sacrifice for, people can either immerse themselves in the pleasurable possibilities of the present moment or look to the past with nostalgia or remorse. It seems to me there's quite a bit of both going on these days. No need to cite specific examples; they're everywhere to be seen. Conservatives and liberals both lament the breakdown of discipline in society today, but who is willing to make sacrifices without a future to hope in?

If you think I'm exaggerating about all this, ask a few Christians what they really hope for their future. I daresay that not one in a hundred will express a desire for sainthood. But why not? Sainthood is the Church's way of affirming the realization of beatific bliss! It is a scandal that we have far more people who want to be corporate executives than we do wanting to be saints!

Again, however, I don't think we've done a good job of promoting sainthood as the ideal to strive for. We tend to portray saints as people who are very different from ourselves in holiness and weirdness! Some of them *were* odd, but they were also very, very happy people who lived life to the fullest. In a world starving for healthy heroes, why have the saints not inspired our hope and imagination? Could it be, again, that we just haven't been very creative and imaginative in teaching about them?

HOPE AND DEATH

Hope has its goal in the future, and the only thing about the future that we can all count on is death. As Pulitzer-Prize–winning author Ernest Becker noted in his book *The Denial of Death*, we all spend a great deal of time denying the fact of our mortality. As spiritual beings who experience self-consciousness, the fact of death seems to be an absurdity. We know there is something about us that transcends space and time, but death seems to be the end of life, at least as we know it. And so we deny death and mortality in order to avoid facing its absurdity.

We cannot deny it completely, however. Friends and family members die, we get older and experience a diminishment in our energies, we hear of accidents that kill young and healthy people. Those who have no hope in heaven experience extreme anxiety whenever the reality of death becomes evident. This anxiety has very deep roots within us, and we work very hard to avoid facing it. Having met with many people in spiritual direction, I am convinced that there is no ultimate resolution to our anxiety about death without something like the hope that Christianity holds out to us.

The great truth revealed to us by Christ is that death is not the end of life but a transition to another, more spiritual mode of existence. If we can accept this as the truth about our death and our future, much of our deep existential anxieties will dissipate. We might even come to think of death not as the great enemy of life but as an essential part of life. From the moment we were conceived, we have been both living and dying. Living means letting go of what has gone before—literally dying to the self that we once were so that we can experience what is yet to come. There are hundreds and hundreds of deaths and resurrections in our lives. This is what Christianity means by the paschal mystery. For something new and wonderful to emerge, that which was there before has to die and give way. Our death will be the last of these experiences of letting go, and we have the revelation of Christ to help us hope in what is to come afterwards.

Of course, there are many who resist the paschal mystery, who want to define themselves according to their own preconceptions, who want to control life and cheat death. That is why, I suppose, the *Catechism* also states that hope includes the "fear of offending God's love and of incurring punishment" (#2090).[4] We've probably emphasized offending God and incurring punishment enough during the history of Christianity, but that doesn't mean we now ought to ignore the topic completely. In one sense, the statement from the *Catechism* is misleading, for it suggests a positive rejection by a disapproving God. God does no such thing, of course. God only loves us; that is all. If we close ourselves to God's love by trying to control life and be self-sufficient, *we cut ourselves off* from the flow of grace that is the divine life in ourselves and creation. It isn't so much that God is offended and therefore punishes us as that we experience consequences for disengaging from the life of God.

While hoping for heaven, then, it is equally important to not take its realization for granted. "Enter through the narrow gate," said Jesus, "for the gate is wide and the road is easy that leads to destruction, and there are many who take it. For the gate is narrow and the road is hard that leads to life, and there are few who find it" (Matthew 7:13-14). Heaven can be lost or postponed longer than we would like: that is what those doctrines on hell and purgatory tell us. Let us therefore hope that we will not delude ourselves and travel the road "that leads to destruction." Instead, may we long for the happiness of the beatific vision. As Christians, let us also teach "what no eye has seen, nor ear heard, nor the human heart conceived, what God has prepared for those who love him" (1 Corinthians 2:9).

~

Reflection and Practice

~ What images come to mind when you consider heaven?

~ How do you feel about sainthood as the goal of your Christian life?

~ How do you feel about the prospect of your death? How do faith and hope enable you to consider your death?

~ Use the affirmation "Jesus, I hope in you" when you feel anxious about death and suffering.

---

1. *Catechism of the Catholic Church*, Liguori, MO: Liguori Publications, 1994, p. 507.
2. Karl Rahner and Herbert Vorgrimler, *Dictionary of Theology*, New York: The Crossroad Publishing Co., 1981, pp. 42-43.
3. *Catechism*, p. 507.
4. *Catechism*, p. 507.